GROWING

yourself UP

First published 2012

Exisle Publishing Pty Ltd
'Moonrising', Narone Creek Road, Wollombi, NSW 2325,
Australia
P.O. Box 60–490, Titirangi, Auckland 0642, New Zealand
www.exislepublishing.com

National Library of Australia Cataloguing-in-Publication Data:

Brown, Jenny, 1959–.

Growing yourself up : how to bring your best to all of life's
relationships / Jenny Brown.

ISBN 9781921497971 (pbk.)

Includes bibliographical references and index.

Interpersonal relations.
Relationship quality.

302

Designed and typeset by Tracey Gibbs
Printed in Shenzhen, China, by Ink Asia

This book uses paper sourced under ISO 14001 guidelines from
well-managed forests and other controlled sources.

10 9 8 7 6 5

Disclaimer
While this book is intended as a general information resource
and all care has been taken in compiling the contents, this
book does not take account of individual circumstances and
is not in any way a substitute for professional advice. Always
consult a qualified practitioner or therapist. Neither the author
nor the publisher and their distributors can be held responsible
for any loss, claim or action that may arise from reliance on the
information contained in this book.

GROWING *yourself* UP

HOW TO BRING YOUR BEST TO ALL OF LIFE'S RELATIONSHIPS

Jenny Brown *MSW*

EXISLE
PUBLISHING

Jenny Brown *is the founder and director of the Family Systems Institute in Sydney, Australia, where she has a counselling practice and trains mental health professionals and organisations. She has trained and earned academic awards at the University of Sydney and Columbia University, New York. Additionally, Jenny has completed many years of post-graduate education in systems approaches to counselling at Relationships Australia, Sydney; the Family Institute of Westchester, New York; and the Tavistock and Portman in London. Jenny lives in Sydney with her husband and two dogs and enjoys keeping in touch with her important relationships, in particular her two adult daughters as they make their way in the world.*

'Jenny Brown has written an extraordinary book on Bowen Theory: clear, easy to read, while maintaining all the human complexity of Bowen's theory of differentiation or maturity. Brown's examples ring true and her clarity on the key points of developing mature relationships with those in your life. The book is a welcome breath of air for all those interested in understanding or conveying to others the principles of managing relationships with spouses, partners, siblings, and others. Every clinician should have copies of this book to give to clients.'
— *Monica McGoldrick, M.A., M.S.W., Ph.D. (Hon), Director of the Multicultural Family Institute in Highland Park, New Jersey; Visiting Professor at Fordham University School of Social Service; and Professor of Clinical Psychiatry at the Robert Wood Johnson Medical School*

'In *Growing Yourself Up*, Jenny Brown demonstrates, through fascinating case vignettes and her own elegant clinical insights, how the challenging task of achieving maturity is possible.'
— *Dr Elliott J. Rosen, Ed.D., Director Emeritus, Family Institute of Westchester, White Plains, New York*

'This book is an excellent resource for those interested in pursuing greater emotional maturity in their relationships (and those learning to help others do so). In short, a wonderfully clear, thoughtful and engaging read. I recommend it highly.'
— *Elizabeth A. Skowron, Ph.D., Associate Professor of Counseling Psychology, Pennsylvania State University*

'This will be a book that readers will return to again and again to refresh their thinking and their efforts to be effectively present and accounted for in the major relationships of their lives.'
— *Dan Papero PhD, MSW, Faculty of The Bowen Center for the Study of the Family, Washington, DC*

'One of the marks of a truly brilliant idea is that once you hear it — especially from an expert — it sounds perfectly obvious. I had exactly this experience reading Jenny Brown's *Growing Yourself Up*. On almost every page I found myself thinking: of course!'
— *Rev Dr John Dickson, Director, Centre for Public Christianity; Senior Research Fellow, Macquarie University, Sydney*

'*Growing Yourself Up* is a book of wisdom, presented carefully and empathically without pulling any punches. The ideas will resonate, not as being from the ivory tower of academia but by reminding us of deep truths that you somehow already know.'
— *Dr Paul Rhodes, Senior Lecturer, Clinical Psychology Unit, University of Sydney*

Contents

Introduction   1
Who's willing to work at growing up?

**Part 1 Understanding the relationship foundations
of adult maturity**

1. Becoming a self in our relationships   11

2. Real maturity or pretend maturity?   26
   How to tell the difference

3. Family ties that bind   37
   Understanding our family of origin

Part 2 Maturity for the first half of adult life

4. Leaving home and growing up   53
   Out into the big wide world

5. The single young adult   66
   Learning how to relate wisely to yourself

6. How marriage can grow people   81
   Changing yourself and not your spouse

7. Sex for grown-ups   97
   Two contrasting bedroom stories

8. Grown-up parenting   106
   Setting an example for the next generation

Part 3 Being a grown-up beyond our family

9. Off to work we go   133
   Maturity gaps in the workplace

10. Developing mature beliefs   150
    Compliance, rebellion or examination

Part 4 Nurturing maturity in the face of setbacks

11. Separation and divorce 165

   Getting beyond blaming

12. Symptoms and setbacks 172

   The uneven playing field of maturity

Part 5 Maturity enhancement in the second half of life

13. Midlife 189

   Crisis or an opportunity for growth?

14. Ageing well 197

   Retirement, the empty nest, relating to a third generation

15. Old age and facing death 206

   Denial or honest preparation

From the inner child to the inner adult 215

Reflections on the lifelong journey of maturity

Epilogue 216

Society and self: the bigger picture of maturity

Appendix 1: Summary questions for reflection 223

Appendix 2: Mature connection and separateness 226

Appendix 3: What are guiding principles? 228

Appendix 4: Differentiation of self as a continuum 231

Notes 233

Bibliography and further reading 237

Acknowledgments 239

Index 241

Who's willing to work at growing up?

Growing maturity, based on seeing the patterns of relationship we're part of, promotes more honesty, humility and improved health for us and for those we care about.

'Grow up!' How many times have you heard this, said it or thought it in times of frustration? Maybe it was said to you, or a brother or sister, by your parents. Perhaps you've said it in a moment of annoyance to one of your kids. Have you thought it of your colleagues at work or of your spouse? It may be that one of your siblings still struggles with the same growing-up problems as an adult that they had as teenagers; or you could be frustrated by your adult children's reluctance to fly the nest.

Perhaps you picked up this book with the idea of giving it to one of these people who 'really needs to get their act together'. This might come from a real sense of caring for another, but the problem is that this focus on others can leave a whopping blind spot when it comes to our own lapses in maturity. We're often prone to thinking that if only that other person could grow up a bit we'd be able to get on with being our own mature selves.

While many of us get caught up in finding fault in others when things seem to go off course, there are some who are always finding fault in themselves: 'I'm the problem in this family'; 'They wouldn't be so upset if I was a better daughter/parent/spouse.' Whether it's judging another or harshly judging ourselves, this pathway doesn't bring lasting growth in us. So what's going to remove these barriers to personal growth? What is the road to adult maturity?

Maturity that grows self, rather than promotes it

The popular answer to this question is to improve yourself by magnifying your good qualities and potential. Have you noticed how approaches to building self-esteem focus on promoting our strengths and avoid looking at the gaps in our maturity? Self-promotion can easily lead to demoting others. If we don't feel happy, it's easy to think that others are standing in our way and causing our unhappiness. It's all too easy to believe that if we can get people to change, or if we could avoid difficult people, perhaps we could then be free to reach our potential.

Many have discovered that this path of inflating the self at the expense of others fails to deliver lasting stability or satisfaction. Each time a new challenge is confronted, the formula of trying to change or blame other people is applied, resulting in a continuous cycle of relationship disappointments. Either we become resentful of others not improving in response to our efforts to help them, or we discard people who disappoint us in the same vein as a pair of shoes that has gone out of style or lost its comfortable fit.

If you're more prone to blaming yourself, the common self-help formula is to correct the negative messages you give yourself and replace them with positives. This can help for a while but seems very hard to maintain in the face of deeply ingrained sensitivities to not measuring up for others.

Relationships, the best place to grow

Whether we see the problem in others or in ourselves, we're likely to miss seeing that each of us is part of a system of relationships that deeply influences each individual's capacity for emotional resilience. Given that our original family has such a profound sway on the development of our maturity, it follows that going back to these formative relationships is the best laboratory in which to make positive changes. Genuine maturity for life starts with learning to observe ourselves in our relationships, and appreciating that problems are not just in the individual but also in the interconnections — the relationship systems — with others.

The project of growing ourselves, our task of seeking to understand how we may be contributing to our own dissatisfactions in our interactions, is all about personal responsibility in our relationships and not about self-promotion. It's a project that can gradually transform even the most challenging of our relationships as our awareness of the effect we have on others, and the way we react to them, increases. Growing maturity, based on seeing the patterns of relationship we're part of, promotes more honesty, humility and improved health for us and for those we care about. This book is about how to develop this awareness and put into action the lessons from it. It's about growing ourselves up and seeing every stage of life as a rich opportunity to facilitate this. Few of us like to think that as adults we still could benefit from a bit more maturity, but when we are willing to be more real about our relating patterns and work to change ourselves, the benefits for us and our relationships can be profound.

Bowen family systems theory

It's important to know where the ideas in this book come from in order to judge their trustworthiness. They're based on a theory developed by psychiatrist and researcher Dr Murray Bowen (1913–90) that is backed up by a growing body of empirical research.[1] In recent years Bowen's concept of 'differentiation of self' — which describes differing levels of maturity in relationships — has been shown by researchers to be related to important areas of wellbeing, including marital satisfaction, and the capacity to handle stress, make decisions and manage social anxiety.

Bowen was a US army physician during World War II who became interested in psychiatry after seeing the varying effects of trauma on soldiers. Bowen's theory is invaluable for helping us to understand the variations in how different people manage similarly stressful circumstances. He originally trained in Freud's psychoanalysis but departed from this theory as he observed that human difficulties went beyond unresolved issues in the individual's psyche and were, rather, embedded in each person's family system — the focus of this book on relationship systems. In researching whole families at the US National Institute of Mental Health in the 1950s, Bowen noticed patterns of managing anxiety in families that were similar to the instinctive ways other species dealt with threats in (or to) their herds and packs. Bowen saw our personal and relationship problems as coming from exaggerated responses to sensing a threat to family harmony and that of other groups. For example, the reaction to a family disagreement can be such an inflated pull for unity that there's no tolerance for differences of opinion. Or an upset in a child is responded to with such an intense effort to protect the child that he or she consequently has no room to develop their own capacity to soothe themselves.

Bowen's concept of differentiation of self forms the basis of this book's description of maturity. The concept of differentiation can be confusing but, put simply, it refers to the ability to think as an individual while staying meaningfully connected to others. It describes the varying capacity each person has to balance their emotions and their intellect, and to balance their need to be attached with their need to be a separate self. Bowen proposed that the best way to grow a more solid self was in the relationships that make up our original families; running away from difficult family members would only add to the challenges in managing relationship upsets.

Bowen is unusual in the field of psychiatry in that he described himself as needing to address the same self-management issues as those his patients were learning to deal with. He didn't think that any human was close to being completely differentiated, and is reported by close colleagues to have said that only on his very best days might he appear to be in the upper to moderate range of emotional maturity.

Bowen's theory doesn't focus on mental illness but on the challenges of being human in the relationships which affect us all. It's not an easy theory to grasp, as it focuses on the big-picture patterns of a system rather than the narrower view of what causes difficulties for one individual. These ideas invite us to see the world through the lens of each family member rather than just from our own subjective experience; they don't allow room for simply seeing victims and villains in our relationship networks. Seeing the system takes people beyond blame to seeing the relationship forces that set people on their different paths. This way of seeing our life challenges avoids fault-finding and provides a unique path to maturing throughout our adult lives.

The road ahead

The chapters ahead will discuss how each stage of the adult life cycle, from leaving home to facing death, provides distinctive opportunities to work on being a bit more differentiated — to be real people in our important relationships. Each chapter contains case studies; some examples will be different to yours while others may sound as if they were written from your own life. The relationship phases explored may not yet fit your lived experience but it's worth taking the time to read these sections as they may still be useful in shedding light on the challenges you may be facing in your current circumstance — and you can be sure that someone significant in your life is going through this life stage. The goal is to not only understand yourself in relationships but to make better sense of how others are shaped by the relationship system.

Part 1 looks at the foundations of adult maturity. What are the aspects of maturity that develop beyond childhood? You'll learn to spot the often subtle difference between faking it and making it, in terms of genuine maturity. Then you'll see how your family of origin influences the trajectory of maturity for you and other family members. Examples of common family patterns are described to help you understand your parents', siblings' and your own maturity gaps and growth possibilities.

Part 2 looks at maturity opportunities in the first half of adulthood. It begins with how the process of leaving home sets the blueprint for our maturity scripts with others. You will learn about the 'people growing' opportunities of being a single young adult, then a spouse in a committed relationship, managing your vulnerabilities in sex and parenting the next generation.

Part 3 looks at the formula for maturing outside our family relationships in the important context of work and in the development of your religious and philosophical beliefs. You will discover more about how you've taken the patterns you learnt from your original family into all other spheres of life, and how you can draw on this awareness to become a more authentic person.

Part 4 addresses how to use your growing understanding of relationship systems to wisely manage significant setbacks such as divorce and symptoms such as depression and anxiety.

Part 5 then moves back to the life cycle and explores maturity opportunities in the second half of life. You'll learn how midlife and ageing can provide unique opportunities to clarify your principles and strengthen your personal integrity. The maturity challenges of becoming a grandparent and facing a life-threatening illness are considered with clear family systems guidelines for wisely negotiating these phases.

*** *** ***

The lessons, from the examples given, show that it's never too late to do some more growing up. You'll learn to mobilise knowledge about your relationship patterns to become a more genuine self in different contexts. The result is improving your ability to share with and listen to others and to stand firmly on the basis of your beliefs and values. The book finishes with reflections on being mature in society at large, reflecting on the profound implications for our communities if more of us were to commit to growing up through all of our adult lives.

Stepping up to the maturity challenge

It goes without saying that life itself can be a wonderful teacher in terms of growing up. With each transition come unique opportunities for experiencing ourselves in less childish ways and clarifying our principles. Every period of change brings a challenge to the previously relied upon securities. We have the opportunity to learn more about why we predictably react immaturely in certain relational situations and how we can choose to behave differently. Life stages help us appreciate how we're never operating in an individual vacuum but always within a system of relationships. In the space between people, where anxieties flow back and forth, we can find clues as to how we relate that go well beyond explanations based on genetic make-up and temperament.

Are there any of us who don't have some growing work to do? All of us have strengths that help build our confidence and are appreciated by those close to us. At the same time all of us have varying degrees of gaps in our ability to maintain healthy relationships and to stay responsible in the many facets of being an adult. Focusing on building our individual strengths might seem like a logical way to increase our maturity but this may miss the subtle ways in which we undermine our own and others' growth. We don't want our vulnerabilities to diminish our capacity to be a force for health and resilience in our relationship systems.

This book starts with the big question: Are you willing to take a fresh look at your own maturity gaps, instead of declaring that another needs to 'grow up'? This might all sound too much like hard work in your already hectic life; yet if there's the chance that this effort can unveil a very different picture of yourself in your relationships, it might just be worth giving this journey a go.

part 1

UNDERSTANDING *the* RELATIONSHIP FOUNDATIONS *of*

adult maturity

Becoming a self in our relationships

'People frequently are willing to be individuals only to the extent that the relationship system approves and permits it.'[1]

—Michael Kerr MD

'The only person we can change and control is our own self. Changing our own self can feel so threatening and difficult that it is often easier to continue an old pattern of silent withdrawal or ineffective fighting and blaming.'[2]

—Harriet Lerner PhD

'My husband doesn't make any effort to show me he cares.'

'I have given everything to my daughter; why can't she get her life together?'

'My parents never encouraged me and now I am suffering for it.'

There's a common thread to the complaints or concerns that many people bring to a counsellor's office. The problem is the other person and everything would be better if that person realised this. Many are often surprised to hear me say that the only change effort that I think is productive is to figure out what can be changed about ourselves. I explain that to improve a relationship, I believe we're best served by working on understanding and making adjustments to our own reactions in relationships. In response to the idea that focusing on self is a worthwhile project, I regularly hear the question, 'Isn't this selfish?' Others protest, 'Isn't it clear that the symptoms or irresponsible behaviour is in the other person?'

Certainly it's easy to see that focusing on self-entitlement at the expense of others is not constructive. But consider how an effort to change another, who is beyond our control or responsibility, is counterproductive: the more we focus on what's wrong with others, the less aware we are of what others have to deal with in relating with us.

The flip side of the coin is the person who always focuses on what's wrong in themselves. This self-blame, a learnt response, is a reaction to an upset in another person that is then personalised. Whether it's trying to change another or blaming ourselves for another's predicament, our viewpoint is narrowed to putting the issue into one individual. The upset arises in our relationship reactions yet we so easily treat the problem as if it's in the one person, and then set about trying to change them or judge them. Any kind of 'change-and-blame dance' can feel like it's about making life improvements, but when you step back and look at the reality, it's hard to see any evidence of 'people growing' going on.

A dose of relationship maturity for everyone

Are any of us really at the peak of maturity? In my own life and in my years of counselling practice, I haven't yet met anyone who wouldn't benefit from maturing a little more to improve their effectiveness and health in life. I would even go so far as to say that every problem brought to counselling could be more easily resolved if the concerned person first looked carefully at how their own instinctive reactions are getting in the way of issues being addressed effectively in connection with others. Whether it's a relationship in strife, an addictive habit, a defiant child or a debilitating anxiety, all these situations would be helped by the presence of thoughtful adults, who expressed themselves responsibly without telling others what to do or waiting for others to fix things for them. The overriding question for growing ourselves up is: Am I up for addressing the immature part I'm playing in my relationships? This question has potential to generate genuine awareness, not a pretend, inflated view of ourselves. Seeing what we need to change about our unhelpful reactions, and working on them in the world of relationships, creates positive ripple effects into the systems we're part of. It can even ripple into future generations.

Figuring out our maturity level when under relationship pressure

The first step to growing a more mature self is to assess where you're starting from. How real is your estimation of your own maturity? I know for myself that I can think I'm pretty grown up when things are relatively calm and in my control; but when a good dose of relationship pressure gets injected into my world, in the blink of an eye my 'inner child' surfaces. This inconsistency in my maturity is seen when in one context I can stand up in front of large audiences and deliver a presentation with poise and confidence, and then find myself the following weekend in the midst of a storm of extended family upset where I lose my ability to speak at all. In one setting I can contain my nervous energy to stay focused on my task; and in a different environment I can't think for myself because I'm caught up in reactions to someone else's upset. One minute I look and feel all grown up and then, in an instant, immaturity jumps to the fore to take centre stage.

Discovering our inner child or growing our inner adult?

Much has been written about how to rediscover our inner child. Maybe the appeal of reclaiming the child within is all about finding the innocence and vulnerability that hasn't been tarnished by the challenges and pains of life. I can see that the playfulness and adventuresome spirit of childhood is worth staying in touch with throughout life. However, there are lots of things about being a child which don't help us through challenges or assist us to fulfil our responsibilities in the varied aspects of life and relationships. Focusing on healing childhood hurts has been given lots of airplay but perhaps we'd be better served if our focus went into growing our inner adult consistently across all areas of our relationships.

To get a clear picture of what it is to be mature, let's take a look at what childhood immaturity looks like. One of the hallmarks of children's energy is the push to get their needs instantly met. The young child hasn't learnt to tolerate waiting for, or being denied, what they want. A two-year-old expects to be instantly gratified. It's as if they want to return to the womb, where being attached to their mother's umbilical cord ensured that everything good was on tap. The toddler's tantrum is always triggered by not getting their way. They insist on having what they want and having it *now!* The trademark of the childish tantrum is that emotions are out of control. Mum has just said no to the request for the chocolate bar on display at the supermarket checkout and the child dissolves into a catastrophic meltdown as if the world were coming to an end. The drama, the decibels and the distress are way out of proportion with the facts of what caused the upset.

The relationship language of childhood

Feelings dominate the life of the child who has not yet developed or learnt to mobilise their thinking brain to solve the problems of life's setbacks. The child's world revolves around finding the fastest route to getting comfortable, to being nurtured and gratified by others. Their focus is on getting what they want from others and not on what they expect of themselves in terms of reasonable behaviour. Have you noticed what the precocious child says when they are denied what they feel entitled to? They cast all their blame on the other and declare they hate that person. My father enjoyed retelling the story of my three-year-old efforts to muster the cruellest tirade I could find in my limited vocabulary, as an act of revenge. I was slighted when my dad stopped me from playing with his shaving equipment. The story goes that I looked him in the eye and said, 'You are a dumb, dumb! You are a pooh, pooh, dumb, dumb!' All of my childhood efforts went into finding the most potent insult to hoist on my father who had denied me my fun with razors and shaving cream.

Another aspect of childhood is doing whatever it takes to get out of unpleasant tasks. The child resorts to whinging until their carer takes over for them rather than persevering with something that doesn't come easily, such as tying shoelaces or packing away toys. On the other hand, if the task of the moment is pleasurable, the child is reluctant to allow another onto this turf to share the fun and the spotlight. They are also appalled at the prospect of having to stop the fun activity when it's time to move on. The child's skills of protest or procrastination in order to prolong self-gratification are impressive.

As the child's brain develops and they become more socially aware, their efforts go towards fitting in and being part of the group.

The fastest route to comfort moves on from having the toy they want to being part of the fun group. Energy goes into being noticed by others and being somebody's best friend, which is of course a very fickle exercise. The older child is easily led by others and changes their tastes frequently in order to be part of the group.

Learning from the child to understand growing up

These characteristics of childhood describe all of us at various times in our lives. Perhaps they embarrassingly describe how we behaved just the other day. It's not just children who let their feelings rule their behaviour and struggle to tolerate delaying their wants. Indeed, adolescents are well known to specialise in many of these childhood tendencies. The self-gratifying, impulsive aspects of childhood are surely not things we want to rediscover and nurture. If we truthfully examine these emotionally driven behaviours we can see that they don't really serve us or those we care about well at all. They might relieve our stress in the short term but don't help us to have the kind of relationships we aspire to.

Having reflected on ways the child responds to discomfort, it's clear that growing up requires a move away from these early life reactions. Childlike impulsiveness for us adults reflects the challenge to contain our emotional reactions and bring them under the guidance of our thinking brains. A key distinguishing factor of being an adult in relationships is having the capacity to see that it's not all about you! We are part of a bigger picture of interconnections between people, where our reactions can either enhance or quash the growing-up space of others.

Attributes of being a mature self in relationships

See what you think of the following checklist in terms of providing a clear picture of what is required to move beyond childhood and to bring the best of your adult self to your relationships.

1. Have your feelings without letting them dominate; tolerate delayed gratification

Mobilising our inner adult means learning how to turn down the intensity of emotional reactions. Instead of letting feelings and impulses dominate, as in the childhood tantrum, we use our adult developed brain to turn down exaggerated feelings so that some logical thinking can occur.

In contrast to the child, the mature adult is recognised by their ability to delay gratification and tolerate hard work, discipline and at times unpleasantness, in order to fulfil responsibilities and achieve goals. A mature adult does not expect others to meet their needs and knows that they should not always expect to be gratified.

2. Work on inner guidelines; refrain from blaming

Discovering our inner adult means finding out what our guiding values and principles are in order to stay clear about how to manage ourselves during demanding times.

The mature person is able to refrain from the childish impulse to blame others when things don't go well. Instead they have learnt to look at themselves first to see what part they have played in the difficulty and what's within their control in order to bring something constructive to the situation. The inner adult refrains from finding fault with another but rather considers how they have contributed to the upset they are in.

3. Accept people with different views; keep connected

Unlike the child who is declaring their rejection of the one who has said no to them, the mature adult is able to stay connected with people who have disagreed or not cooperated with them. Rather than shut off, retaliate or distance themselves from those who have upset them, the grown-up is able to stay in communication with others in the face of disagreements.

4. Be responsible for solving your own problems

Another contrast to the child's way of operating is that the mature adult does not expect others to solve their problems or step in to take over when tasks are demanding. Maturity is illustrated by not inviting others to take over our own responsibilities or insecurities. It also means not jumping in to do this for others when we see them struggling. *Learning how not to do for others what they can learn to do for themselves is one of the golden rules of adult maturity.* This rule is crucial if we don't want to become a hindrance to others reaching their grown-up potential. Even when we have skills that allow us to do a more efficient job than another, it's far from a caring act to take over and crowd another's space, quashing their ability to find their own way through their tasks. The person who jumps in to rescue others is usually covering over their own insecurities at another's expense. They enjoy feeling the pride of accomplishment beyond their own responsibility while the other is left feeling dependent on them.

5. Hold onto your principles

In relationship to others, the grown-up does not need to be a chameleon who finds comfort by fitting in with the group. They are able to hold their course based on what they believe is right, even when there's pressure to change back to old ways of accommodating and maintaining the status quo.

6. See the bigger picture of reactions and counter-reactions

For the upset child it is all about 'me' — the world is expected to grind to a halt in order to respond to the discomfort in the one individual. The adult can learn to see how their point of view might be very different from others who are relating with them. They can look beyond their own upsets to see how they affect others in the flow of impulses that are a part of human relationships. Rather than shouting 'What about me!' the mature adult is thoughtful in reflecting on 'How are we all impacting each other?'

* * *

What do you think of these characteristics of a truly mature person? Does any of this sound easy? Can you think of the last time your reactions to a stressful situation fell short of these standards of maturity? To what extent do you find it possible to maintain the characteristics of the inner adult who:

» keeps their emotions in line with their values;

» stays on task even when experiencing discomfort;

» improves themselves without blaming others;

» stays in contact with those who are upset with them;

» doesn't expect to be rescued by others and refrains from taking over for others;

» resists the forces to fit in with the group ethos when it contradicts their values;

» sees beyond self to the patterns of reactions each person is part of?

Most of us can get some of these things right when we're in our comfort zones. The problem emerges when stress levels increase and we revert to parts of our inner child in seeking the fastest path to our own ease. I recall the stress of feeling like a stranger at university and how this increased my tendency to go along with the popular group in order to fit in. I quickly changed my political views to fit the majority in my classes and I was vague about my religious views with those I sensed would disapprove. Under the pressure of adjusting to university life in my late teens, my immaturities came to the fore.

The biology of growing up

Isn't growing up just a natural occurrence? But wait one minute! Before thinking any further about attaining relational maturity it's worth asking the question: isn't growing up inevitable as we age and gain more experience? Indeed, it's the case that much of our growing up just happens of its own biological accord. Without any effort or initiative our bodies and minds grow in size and complexity and then inevitably, as the years progress, they start to degenerate. We don't choose for this to happen and can't halt its progress in spite of a huge industry that promises to delay the ageing process.

Many of the childhood behaviours already described can be understood in terms of brain development. Here is a simplified crash course in developmental neuroscience. Young children make decisions from part of the brain called the amygdala, which is primarily the emotional centre of the brain. This means that actions are determined strongly from emotional impulses, and gradually as a child grows they are able to draw more from the prefrontal cortex, which enables reasoning. Teenagers are known to have only part of this prefrontal dominance developed, which means they can draw from their reasoning when things are calm but can easily get flooded with emotional responses when there are multiple stimuli and stress is high.

While the brain increases its capacity for complex decision-making as a person enters their twenties, experience tells us there is no guarantee that adults will always be able to make wise decisions, especially during times of stress. Each day in the marketplace, on the roads and in social groups, we notice there's a huge variance in people's ability to maintain clear thinking when aroused by some kind of aggravation. One of the challenges to our growing up is that our lower brain (the amygdala) has stronger connections to our upper thinking brain (the prefrontal cortex) than is the case in the reverse direction. This means it's easier for us to let our emotions rule our thinking; and it takes a more concerted effort for us to gain conscious control over our anxious reactions. It takes practice to shift the 'bottom up' emotional tendency of our brain to more of a 'top down' thoughtful brain. The good news from neuroscience is that the brain is not fixed in its capacities when adulthood begins, it's far more flexible than previously thought, with an extraordinary capacity to build new strengths and repair itself. A variety of relationship experiences gives the brain an expanded capacity to cope with social challenges. This creates a compelling imperative to be proactive in growing our brains. Far from being set in stone by the time childhood ends, our neurological pathways are responsive to our choices about how we manage our stress responses and how we handle a range of different relationships.

Growing up relationally

While much physical growing doesn't require effort, growing emotionally in the area of relationships is a very different process. Have you witnessed young people who demonstrate wisdom beyond their years? They're able to say what they think even when the pressure to fit in with the group is high. Have you also observed some adults, with decades of life experience, who appear to behave as reactively as a two-year-old having a tantrum? Their innate emotions dominate their thinking and they inject such a charge of anxiety into situations that it's hard to see the facts of what's going on. My experience of life tells me that there are times when I can behave in quite mature ways, rising to the occasion and demonstrating impressive clarity and speed of thinking, even in the midst of a crisis. Then at other times I disappoint myself, and others, by behaving impulsively. I'm the same individual in each situation but the relationship conditions are always changing and impacting my degree of maturity.

We can all see that even though an elderly person may have lots of life experience wisdom to draw from, this doesn't guarantee their maturity. Many older people carry throughout their lives the same inner-child impulses they left home with. This book aims to shed light on this puzzle of why growing up in relationships can be so erratic and challenging. It will also tackle the question: what can we do to lend a hand to our biology in becoming more mature adults?

Relationships, the best laboratory for growing up

If we're to lift our maturity levels from what we had when we left our family homes, a conscious, persistent effort is required. The very best place to work on growing that inner adult, rather than pandering to that entitled inner child, is in our significant relationships. Where else do we get such good practise at using the characteristics of the inner adult than in relating to important people in our lives? Do you recall the last big family event you attended? There are few better contexts in which to find opportunities to practice keeping our exaggerated reactions in check than the gathering of relatives celebrating a significant ritual.

The driver of childish ways in relationships is our instinct to relieve any presence of discomfort in ourselves. So much of our discomfort is about relationships: not fitting in, not getting enough attention, not feeling able to meet expectations, not feeling adequate to help another in distress. I have learnt to see how subtle my efforts to relieve discomfort are and how these efforts have a cost for others in my life as well as myself. Recently one of my adult daughters talked to me about a struggle she was having. I had earlier noticed that she seemed to be tracking really well, which helped me to feel comfortable. At the mention of an old struggle I noticed that I immediately felt my mood drop. I felt depleted and flat as if the struggle was mine and not hers. My automatic response to relieve my distress would be either to take on the job of trying to solve her problem for her by giving advice, or to move into a cocoon of distance where I would relate more superficially and make less contact. I can kid myself that my advice-giving comes from generous empathy or that my stepping back is to honour her need to be independent, but at the bottom of each response is my instinct to make myself feel a bit better. Over the years I've learnt to better recognise my predictable automatic ways to relieve my discomfort. In my interaction with my daughter I remind myself of what being grown up in this relationship looks like. Rather than advising, I show an interest in all aspects of what she's been doing and make sure that I really listen and keep contact with her and share what's happening in my life, not as a mother who feels her daughter's emotions as if they were my own but as a separate person in real contact with her. These same principles relate to my efforts in my marriage, with work colleagues and with other family members.

Tolerating a 'go slow' approach

You've probably figured out by now that the message of this book isn't about miracle pathways to growing up. It's based on the view that, with a willingness to go slowly and learn about yourself in different relationships, it's possible to tone down immature ways of relating that get in the way of yours and others' progress. In a recent counselling session, a middle-aged woman wisely declared: 'I used to get impatient about my slow progress but I now see that being more effective and mature in life is like running a marathon.'

From my experience, and that of countless people I have had the privilege to work with, I believe there are no short sprints to growing up. Hence it's wise to be aware of overambitious attempts to change at once everything that you see as immature about yourself. If, however, you're already seeing that maturity is about a willingness to work on yourself, rather than the common path of focusing on the faults of others, then you can take heart that your energies are directed towards progress.

It's also useful to consider your motivation for improving your maturity. If your efforts are driven by a self-centred desire to be admired and to have all your needs and wants met in relationships, you're likely to get stuck with your immature inner child. If, on the other hand, you're motivated by a desire to bring the best of yourself to the lives of those who are important to you and to bring some maturity to the communities in which you live, you're likely to be freer to grow.

Questions for reflection

» In what relationship situations do I see my impulsive 'inner child' come through?

» Which aspects of my inner adult would I like to see more of:

    a) keeping feelings from getting exaggerated;

    b) working on being more principled, not on blaming others;

    c) becoming more comfortable relating to people who disagree with me;

    d) being responsible for myself without interfering in others' responsibilities;

    e) being able to stand on my values even when I won't be popular;

    f) being able to see past myself to the bigger picture of reactions and counter-reactions?

» Am I up for working on addressing the immature part that I'm playing within my network of relationships?

It may be helpful when considering these questions to refer to Appendix 3 for some examples of guiding principles.

2.

Real maturity or pretend maturity?

How to tell the difference

'It is average for the human to "pretend" a state [of maturity] which has not been attained. In certain situations, every person is vulnerable to pretending to be more or less mature than he or she really is.'[1]

—Murray Bowen MD

'The pseudo-self is an actor and can be many different selfs. The list of pretends is extensive. He can pretend to be more important or less important, stronger or weaker, or more attractive or less attractive than is realistic.'[2]

—Murray Bowen MD

Before starting work on being more mature it's worth being aware that it's possible to achieve a fake kind of maturity in relationships. All of us have some degree of pretend maturity in our repartee of relating. We're prone to doing a patch-up job on the immaturity blocks we inherit from the generations of our families' anxious sensitivities so that they're hidden from view as much as possible. Any patching up that we do can make us look pretty impressive at times as we switch on our most confident persona. This counterfeit type of maturity is not always unhelpful as it enables us to rise to many challenges in life and cope beyond our usual capacities. This 'winging it' kind of maturity can be an adaptive advantage, but it can also be a bit of a trap in giving us an inflated view of our maturity. We might miss the opportunity to see ourselves more realistically and address our maturity shortfalls.

One of the best ways to test the genuineness of your inner adult is to see if the characteristics of maturity are displayed in each part of your life. This means that we are able, in *all* of our relationship contexts — not just at work or with the children or in our marriage, or with our friends or in our community, or with each member of our family of origin — to have reasonable success in:

» keeping our emotions in line with our principles;
» staying on task even when facing obstacles;
» working on improving ourselves and not blaming others;
» staying in contact with those who disagree with us;
» not looking to others to bail us out of our problems;
» refraining from taking over for others;
» resisting the force to change ourselves in order to be accepted by the group.

This ideal applies to not just the easy parts of our life but also where things are more tense or when we are away from the public gaze. To be genuinely grown up we will tackle our immature tendencies in all aspects of life: at home, at work, in the community, with extended family — and even in the midst of traffic congestion!

Jerry's story of inconsistent maturity

Many people appear to be quite mature in their public profiles yet struggle to lift themselves above childish tendencies in their home lives. An example of this was Jerry, who came to counselling reeling from the distress of his wife Sally walking out on him. This shockwave came after 30 years of marriage and the raising of four children to adulthood.

Jerry said in a somewhat stunned state: 'I have always been an optimist, believing that nothing bad would happen to me and if a problem arose I'd always be able to find my way through it. I can't believe that Sally is refusing to come back and to work on our marriage!'

In his current circumstances Jerry was reduced to a distressing state of helplessness. Sally had told him that in her heart she had left the marriage years ago and she had only remained for the stability of the children. Jerry described his desperation in pleading with Sally to try to work things out, only to be met by her resolute declaration that it was too late now as she had lost all motivation to try. Jerry could not come to terms with the lack of options he had in trying to pull his marriage together.

In desperation he asked, 'How could she do this to me, and to our kids? Doesn't she realise how much this will damage us all and the family's reputation? At least she could have given me some forewarning!'

As Jerry began to reflect on himself as a husband, he started to acknowledge that he had neglected his wife in many ways and had taken her commitment for granted. The biggest conundrum for Jerry was that intellectually he knew that a good marriage required regular times to talk, attention to a healthy sex life and working together on managing the household and parenting; yet Jerry had behaved in ways that contradicted his own beliefs. He had been a high flyer in his law practice and was admired by many. Over the years he had mentored younger associates with marriage problems, and he had even given them advice about how to get a better work–life balance.

As Jerry emerged from behind his shock and denial he started to ask himself, 'How could I have been so wise with others and so stupid in my own marriage?'

Jerry was facing the jarring realisation that his seemingly mature persona in the outside world had not translated into a depth of principled living in one of the most important arenas of his life. He expressed his heartbreak in realising this now, when it appeared it was too late to turn things around in his marriage. Of course, there were many patterns of immaturity in his wife Sally that led her to being secretive about her discontent. It was appealing for Jerry to focus on his wife's failings but when questioned he could acknowledge that this would do him no good in addressing his own immaturity.

Jerry is not alone with this problem of inconsistency. He knew how to function with responsibility in some parts of his life but neglected his responsibility in other important areas. When he had a public audience he was able to feed off the validation this gave him to build a strong façade; but when he was behind the scenes he was unable to find the drive to pursue his values. His behaviour was directed more by what was rewarding and comfortable in the here and now than what he believed was important and would bring longer term satisfaction.

Staying where it's uncomfortable in relationships

To varying degrees, all of us have aspects of Jerry's problem: a disparity between what we know is best and how we actually live. Rather than address our immaturity, it's often easier to just focus on doing what brings instant validation and ignore the areas where we have to face up to the disapproval or challenge of others. In this way we borrow a pretend maturity from relationships that validate us rather than grow our inner maturity to become more balanced and responsible across the spectrum of life. We gravitate to the people who admire us and don't threaten to expose our vulnerabilities, and distance ourselves from the important people with whom we have difficult issues to work through. Choosing to avoid tension and stay in situations where we experience more positive energy from others is an attractive path to follow. But it's a path that will restrict our growth, and that of others, towards real maturity.

To stand up as an individual in a relationship requires tolerating episodes of disharmony and disapproval. It's really hard to do this and really easy to just avoid the effort and continue to gravitate towards less threatening relationships. The hard work of becoming more of a defined individual in a relationship, rather than one who tries to blend in, should not be confused with being a rugged individual who doesn't need anyone and goes around defiantly offending family members. Giving up the pull for 'togetherness approval' is very different from giving up the importance of being emotionally close to others.

'Borrowing' maturity

When we rely on pretend maturity to be adults, we learn to be who we think others expect us to be; or alternatively to rebel against the pressure of what we think is expected of us. Complying with others' expectations or rebelling by going in the opposite direction, are both examples of borrowing from relationships to try to be grown up. In contrast, the solid inner adult expresses themselves without using others' approval or disapproval levels to edit who they are.

I don't have to look far to see the ways that I borrowed a self from others in my early adult years. I gained much of myself from my position in the family as my mother's support and confidante. Previously I had been the focus of her anxious concern about my childhood health problems, but as this worry focus shifted to other siblings, I found myself in a perceived place of importance to my mother and translated the confidence this gave me (a kind of borrowed confidence) into roles of leadership in the outside world. As I began to achieve academically and in school leadership positions, I sensed my parents' pride and enjoyed the validation and steadying affect of occupying such a position in my family. During this phase of life I was borrowing some of my pretend maturity from the pride my parents invested in me. And because systems thinking is about how both sides of the relationship affect each other, it's important for me to remember that my parents, too, were steadying parts of themselves through the way they invested in me.

While there's nothing wrong with experiencing the pleasure of a parent's response to our accomplishments, when this becomes the means for bolstering a sense of self, it lessens a person's resilience during times when praise is not forthcoming. It also primes a person to step in and take the stage from others who might benefit from having a role in leadership functions. This is how 'borrowing a self from a relationship' impairs the functioning of someone else in the family who has less space to develop their own strengths and flexibility by managing in different situations.

In my twenties I continued to work hard in my university studies. I had started a law degree and found I felt completely out of place amongst fellow students; I subsequently transferred to social work studies, which felt like a better fit. I was completely oblivious to the reality that my original choice of study was determined more by the viewpoints of others than from thinking for myself about my life and career goals. While the decision to study law was largely influenced by the group around me, my move to social work was driven more by wanting something familiar than by thoughtfully investigating the career options available. The comfort of studying social work was partly an emotional reaction and not simply a choice. I'd found a career path that matched my adolescent family role of pleasing and helping others.

Much of the maturity I was forging was superficial in that it relied upon meeting the perceived expectations of those around me. At times I was able to change like a chameleon to fit into different social contexts and to use my intellect to protect myself from experiencing too much vulnerability. The artificial additions to my sense of maturity served me adequately, although cracks would appear as my vulnerability surfaced at stress points, such as the birth of children. A giant shockwave to my illusion of authentic maturity occurred at age 33 when I faced the death of my second parent. My mother had died of breast cancer when I was 21 and I had avoided being crushed by grief primarily through focusing on having my needs met in my relationship with my soon-to-be husband. When my father died, twelve years later, I confronted an overwhelming sense of emptiness as I contemplated the loss of a parent whom I could make proud. I was about to complete postgraduate study but I no longer felt that my success carried any meaning. This realisation brought my superficial maturity into clear view. My focus for achieving growth was heavily weighted on meeting the expectations of my parents and any relationship that had 'parent-like' qualities. In coming to see that much of my imagined maturity was borrowed from others' approval, I was able to see that I had a lot of growing up to do.

Pretend bravado

When we rely on borrowed maturity we're often able to function at a high level but are dependent on the support of the group to look good. When others focus on our weaknesses we can be easily deflated in our coping abilities. When we operate as a pretend grown-up it's hard to express opinions that might put us out of step with the group. The exception is a rebel-type of pretend bravado which defines us not by pleasing others, but by rebelling and triggering disharmony. Many people shore up a pretend maturity by choosing the opposite position to parents and more mainstream opinion. Just as complying with another is done without much thought, so rebelling can be more of a 'relationship resection' than a carefully researched standpoint. Rebelling can be driven by a desire to belong (to a group of fellow rebels) as much as going along with the majority is driven by the desire for group harmony.

Checklist of the 'surface level' adult

It can be difficult to bring our counterfeit areas of maturity to our awareness. They become such a natural part of our programming that it is often hard to see how they are letting us, and others, down. To begin to recognise pretend maturity, have a look at the checklist below, which outlines characteristics of the superficial or 'surface level' adult, and compare it to the characteristics of real self-esteem, an inner maturity, that doesn't borrow from others' approval or disapproval:

> » Knowledge and beliefs are copied from others rather than thought through for ourself. Life principles are picked up randomly when under pressure and are therefore often inconsistent.

» Beliefs and values can quickly change when relationships feel destabilised. Changes happen in order to enhance our image with another or to oppose others.

» Feeling is more important than thinking in forming our opinions, so that they're expressed with exaggerated assurance, submissive compliance or rebellious opposition.

» There's a degree of pretence in our superficial adult: pretending to be more or less important than we really are, or more or less intelligent, or stronger or more vulnerable than we are.

» Superficial maturity is driven to either seek intense harmony or rugged individuality.

» At times of high stress, our superficial adult uses pleasing others or distancing to relieve tension.

» When maturity is at a surface level, our reactions can occur impulsively as a way of reducing the discomfort generated by intense feelings.

Checklist of the 'solid inner' adult

Now take a look at this checklist of the characteristics of a genuine maturity, an inner maturity that doesn't borrow from others' approval or disapproval:

» The solid inner adult is made up of inner convictions that have been formed gradually and can only be changed from within, not from relationship pressure.

» He or she is able to express a viewpoint clearly without declaring a dogmatic rightness and disinterest in listening to others' views.

» He or she is able to balance working on independent goals with seeking and nurturing closeness with others.

» In times of high stress, the solid inner adult is able to stay connected with others without losing their ability to voice their different viewpoints.

» He or she is able to tolerate intense feelings in themself and others without an impulsive drive to alleviate those feelings.

» He or she is able to focus on self and their part when a difficulty arises in a relationship.

» He or she is able to take responsibility for managing their own anxieties without needing to take responsibility for the feeling states of others.[3]

I find such a list daunting and humbling to read as it exposes my shortfalls in maturity. Before you give up and consign this book to gather dust, be reassured that this list is an ideal that isn't achieved consistently by even the most impressive adults. Most of us can recognise that we have a mixture of both solid and superficial characteristics. The comparison between real self and pretend self can be most helpful in assisting us to have an honest estimation of our maturity. It can help us to be a bit more of an observer of ourselves in our relationships so that we can think about how we want to change and become clearer about what we stand for. It can help us to see when relationship forces take over our thinking for ourselves. We get to see our areas of learnt laziness and our fears of losing harmony with others.

Thinking about the family in which we grew up is a great place to figure out our maturity shortfalls; not so that we gather ammunition to blame our parents, but so we can appreciate their struggles as similar to our own. Knowing our self and our family better gives our inner adult its best chance to grow.

Questions for reflection

» In what parts of my life do I appear most mature? How do I
depend on others' approval to be comfortable in these areas?
» In what parts of my life am I least responsible? Where could I
start to be more of a solid adult in these areas?
» When are the times I look to others to figure out how to behave
as opposed to drawing on my knowledge of myself?

Family ties that bind

Understanding our family of origin

'Gaining more knowledge of one's distant families of origin can help one become aware that there are no angels and devils in a family: they were human beings, each with their own strengths and weaknesses, each reacting predictably to the emotional issue of the moment, and each doing the best they could with their own life course.'[1]

—Murray Bowen MD

'Failing to connect with your family leaves you alone in important ways that lovers, children, friends, and work cannot replace.'[2]

—Monica McGoldrick PhD

How do you think your original family has influenced how grown up you are? The way our parents responded to our childhood expressions of protest and neediness can shed plenty of light on how much space we had to begin to develop our inner adult.

At the risk of simplifying the many factors that go into family dynamics, let's consider a few examples of the influence of various patterns that develop between parents and children. If we were the child whom a parent worried most about, we get accustomed to the emotional pattern of having them jump in to smooth out our difficulties. As a result we instinctively expect and invite others to solve our problems. If one or both of our parents' anxieties were detoured onto perceiving negative attributes in us, it's likely that we got used to exaggerated criticism and correction and could be prone to similar negative overreactions. If a parent reduced their tensions by giving in to our demands from our childhood tantrums we may find it harder to let go of always feeling entitled. If a parent confided or leant on us when things were tough or distant in their marriage, we're likely to be at ease with giving advice, but less comfortable accepting it from others. If we were given centre stage by a parent who secured themself by applauding our achievements in an exaggerated way, we'll struggle as adults to tolerate not being important.

It isn't that our parents cause our limitations but rather that we respond to them in ways that keep these circular patterns going. Our parents' responses to us are as patterned as our instinctual responses to their anxious reactions. The energy we pick up from what our parents convey to each other in their marriage is also a big part of this influential circuitry. We all grow up in families with the backdrop of many generations of patterns that enabled the survival of the group. The parent–child relationship is one of these circuits that sit within a bigger multigenerational tapestry — one that includes dealing with the previous generation of parents, trying to stabilise a marriage and relating to support systems in the outside world.

Each sibling experiences a different family

To appreciate the influence of our original families it's helpful to consider the different maturity pathway each of our brothers and sisters experienced in their growing up. Have you ever paused to appreciate that each of your siblings experienced a different family to you due to the variations in the degree and tone of attention each received from your parents? Some siblings get a balanced amount of attention and assistance in line with their logical needs, while others get an exaggerated degree of positive or negative attention. In this sense we don't grow up with the same experience and perception of our parents as each of our sisters and brothers.

The nature of the attention we get may relate to our sibling position. If you're an eldest of either sex it's likely that you were applauded more for your responsible efforts. This means that your growing up is connected with getting ahead and being a leader who looks for the praise of others. If you followed a sibling whom your parents found especially difficult, it's likely that you responded with heightened compliance and avoidance of upsetting others. Or if you're the youngest in the family it may well be that you became accustomed to being mollycoddled and led by others; if always related to as the baby of the family it's easy to expect that others should pave your way. Decision-making and initiative may be more difficult for the youngest siblings as adults. The 'only child' has the double edge of getting all of their parents' positive focus as well as their worry focus. They may be more likely to expect to be focused on by their superiors and may struggle to direct their life course if this attention is not forthcoming.

None of these sibling roles is set in stone. The sibling position of each parent, for example, will impact on how they relate to each of their children. The useful thing to appreciate in your growing-up efforts is that you can't have the same expectations of each sibling that you have of yourself. Each family member's pathway to maturity is inevitably different from your own.

Beyond blaming our parents

As you begin to think about your family experience you might be casting culpability in your parents' direction. Before pointing the blame finger, pause to consider the place each parent held in their family: how were their pathways to maturity shaped by how their own parents related to them and by the challenges their family faced? This will help you to see your parents as human beings rather than being hasty in labelling them as saints or villains. Much of a parent's reaction to each of their children comes out of an unconscious effort to relieve their own uncertainties and anxiety, not from a deliberate attempt to mess up their children. Our mothers and fathers came out of their own families with a level of tolerance for upset, discord, involvement and demands. In turn this is played out in their marriage and their reactions to each of their children. None of us, or our parents, has any say in the hand of maturity cards we are dealt as part of the inheritance of generations of families.

Greg's story

Greg came to counselling to get help with what he termed his 'commitment phobia'. He walked into my office somewhat awkwardly not having sought any counselling before. His height and smart business attire belied his nervousness as he began to explain that at age 44, his long-term girlfriend Kerry was getting frustrated about his avoidance of the subject of marriage. This was not the first time a girlfriend had lost patience with Greg's avoidance of making plans for the future of the relationship: there had been two earlier long-term relationships that had ended painfully over the same issue. Greg wondered if he could ever grow up when it came to relationships. He said he wanted to be married and have kids and was getting anxious about losing his chance with Kerry.

'I start the relationship with such passion,' he explained, 'but before too long I look for every fault imaginable with these really decent women. What's wrong with me?'

I asked him how he understood what was getting in the way of him taking the step of marriage. He replied, 'I just don't know how to have watertight assurance that I could be happily married forever to Kerry.'

Greg sensed that his anxieties about committing were not all about Kerry. A friend had suggested to him that his relationship fears were caused by an experience of early abandonment by his mother. He had recounted a story he'd heard of how his mother had left him for two weeks with an aunt in his first year of life. At his friend's suggestion Greg had spoken to his mother about the damage this might have caused him. Her response was saturated with enormous guilt as she recounted the story of her difficulty coping with her colicky first baby and the lack of support she received from her husband. Defensively she recounted how a baby health centre nurse had suggested that a couple of weeks' respite would be a good idea. As Greg reflected on this short period of separation when he was well cared for, he was sceptical that this episode could account for the growing-up roadblock he was now trying to negotiate. 'I just can't make sense of how a two-week separation from my mother, that I've no memory of, really cuts it as an explanation for my anxiety about getting married. I don't really buy the idea of this being all about a childhood wound.'

It would be easy to hold Greg's parents responsible for this disruption. His fears of commitment could be blamed on his anxiety about being abandoned again. But this simplified cause-and-effect explanation doesn't leave much room for Greg to grow himself up and to see what he can work on doing differently in his relationships with both his parents. In our efforts to bring out our inner adult by not focusing on others but addressing what we can change in ourselves, it's unproductive to blame one event from the distant past as the single cause of a current relationship impasse.

The problem isn't abandonment but intensity

Greg did get past the potential of blaming this childhood event. He began to examine more broadly his growing-up experiences, which yielded some practical insights.

I asked Greg, 'What do you recall about your parents' relationship?'

He answered: 'My parents had a pretty bad marriage. I have no idea how they are still together after 45 years. My mother has never stopped complaining about how Dad lets her down; but you know what's really weird, I can never remember them having a fight!'

'Can you explain more about how each parent and you related during your growing up?' I asked.

Greg recalled, 'For as long as I can remember, Mum was always talking to me. I don't think Dad was ever there for her and she must have been lonely. I liked being special to her for most of the time but it all got a bit much for me as I got older. I'm still close to Mum but I also get resentful about how much she leans on me.'

'And what about your dad?'

Greg continued to reflect. 'Oh Dad and I were always awkward and distant. I resented how much time he spent at work. My sister Veronica got on better with Dad. She had problems with Mum, though. They were fighting all the time when she was at high school about her dodgy friends and breaking curfew; funny that I never gave Mum or Dad any trouble. Veronica on the other hand was quite a rebel. And she couldn't get out of home fast enough. She still lives as far away as she can; but it's the opposite for me. I have never moved out of the same suburb as Mum and Dad.'

Can you identify some of the patterns of relating Greg developed in his family that form part of his current dilemmas? When asked this very question, after thinking through the facts of his family relationship story, Greg began to piece together some useful insights.

'I've only known how to do relationships one way, where I do all the listening but never say anything about what's going on for me. It's always one-sided with Mum and empty with Dad. I get so intense quickly in my relationships, trying to make the other happy. No wonder I get overwhelmed with Kerry and then distance myself. I guess this is just what my father used to do?'

Putting the relationship puzzle together

Over a period of some months, Greg put effort into getting to know his parents' story of their early adult lives. He also worked at being more open with each of them about what was happening in his life. Greg discovered that his parents, like many other young adults, felt insecure with each other as they embarked on the challenging journey of parenting. In listening to their descriptions of how they adjusted to new responsibilities, Greg could appreciate how his mother coped by putting her focus onto her son to fill the distance that was growing in the marriage. Meanwhile, his father relieved his uncertainty through his distance and avoidance of upsetting his wife.

Greg could see that his mother's focus on him contributed to both a sense of suffocation and a strong dependence. For many years he had fostered this closeness by seeking his mother out and soliciting her attention with his humour. Greg's clash of feeling both dependent and needing space had primed him to be ambivalent in intimate relationships, where he had not grown his ability to develop a separate sense of self.

Maintaining balance

There are patterns and tensions in Greg's family that all of us encounter. Greg, and each member of his family, struggled to get the balance right between their desire for closeness and intimacy and the need for separateness, for some space to be an individual. The ability to be both a distinct self and part of a close relationship is at the core of being able to grow our genuine adult maturity. The maturity blocks come when some family members put all their effort into getting close, and others put their energy into individuality. This common 'pursue and withdraw' division of labour in a relationship can be seen in Greg's parents' marriage and the pattern that he was caught in with Kerry. Being mature means that a person learns to be comfortable and take initiative to be warmly connected as well as being able to operate independently.

When family members struggle to deal with the tension of feeling alone versus feeling smothered they often detour from growing up by getting their needs met in a third-party relationship. This is clearly what occurred when Greg's mother stopped pursuing her husband for closeness and replaced it with an emotional connection with her son. Greg's dad was part of creating this triangle by getting comfortable in his distancing position. He would likely have felt relief and less insecurity about meeting his wife's expectations when she refocused onto their son.

Relationship triangles — an easy detour

Learning to see a triangle forming in a group is one of the most useful tools to avoiding immaturity pitfalls. A relationship triangle is where tensions between two people are relieved by escaping to a third party. This detour to a third helps relieve tension in relationships and in this way it helps families to manage. But it also means that issues between two people stay unaddressed and this tension can become a challenge for another person in the family. Identifying this triangling process within his own family helped shed light on how Greg's parents' marriage was less strained when his mother focused on her son. Greg was able to see that his position as an ally for his mother in her distant marriage had been formative in his style of relating as an adult.

Greg's understanding of his programmed style of relating in a relationship triangle, as a third party in his parents' marriage, helped him to understand and address his difficulties committing to Kerry. When he recognised the significance of his triangle role, Greg immediately set about stopping his detouring to others regarding his concerns about Kerry and found ways to discuss them directly with her. There has been enormous anxiety about whether the relationship with Kerry can sustain this honest person-to-person communication, but Greg has come to see clearly the importance of trying to break the pattern of relating that has been absorbed from his family of origin. When Greg could understand his reactions in relationships, he was less afraid of committing to marriage with Kerry. He reported to me after he proposed to a delighted Kerry that, 'I no longer need a guarantee that Kerry's my perfect match, because I have more awareness to get through the difficult times that will be ahead. If I can keep my stuff in my relationship with Kerry, I'm pretty confident we can make a good go of things.'

Figuring out your triangle detour

Identifying how we might have been involved in such triangles is useful for awareness about how we're prone to taking sides or getting in the middle of other people's issues and avoiding addressing our own. Our triangle positions can be identified by considering who we sided with about another person, or which two people aligned together to focus on us. The triangle that shapes us most is usually the one we occupied with each parent. Other influential triangles can be with one of our parents and a grandparent or a parent and one of our siblings. We may have played the part of an ally with a parent, whom we viewed as being treated badly by the other party; we may have responded as a rescuer or mediator, compelled to look after the needs of both parties; or we may have absorbed the worry focus as the scapegoat or sick one, who provided a kind of glue for another relationship by providing a common cause to unite around. If you were reacted to as the troublemaker or sick one in a triangle with your parents, the growing-up challenge is to learn to express your responsible side. If you were an ally or rescuer for another in your family, a gap you may need to address is learning how to experience and express your vulnerable side.

It may be difficult to see the triangles in your family, as they may only be evident at times of heightened stress. Think back to times when family harmony was put to the test or when a stressful event intensified a mother's or father's need for togetherness or separateness. Often triangles come to the surface when relationships are required to make adjustments, with new additions to the family or family members leaving home. Who did you move towards or away from at these times? Did you move into a position of increased compliance, rebellion or neediness?

The more you're able to see the patterns of triangles that impacted you, the more you will be able to understand your own part in being a conduit to helping problems escape from the relationships they belong in.

An overview of Bowen family systems theory

Given how much this book is about applying Bowen's theory to understanding the commonalities of the families we all grow up in, it's timely to pause and have a crash course in family systems concepts. You will recognise them, described in everyday language, all the way through this book.

Bowen researched his own family over the generations and came to see similarities in coping patterns with those families with more severe psychiatric symptoms. He noticed that there were two forces at work in relationships that drive predictable patterns of behaviour: these are the togetherness force and the separateness force, which are both essential for individuals in their relationships. The core concepts of Bowen's theory describe the ways that family members react to the threat of loss of togetherness and explain the variations in how different families and individuals manage life challenges. These core concepts are: *triangles*, which describe how tension between two people gets detoured to a third party, such as when a wife discusses marital grievances with a friend rather than their husband or when a parent discuss parental grievances with a child rather than their partner; *differentiation of self*, which describes the extent to which family members can stay in their own skin — maintain their individuality — while relating to each other and still being part of the family group; *fusion*, the opposite of differentiation of self, where boundaries are lost in the pull for family togetherness; the *nuclear family emotional system*, which outlines the three ways that one generation of a family can reduce individual relationship discomfort — these are the conflict-and-distance pattern, the over- and under-functioning exchange between spouses, and the anxious detour onto a child. The *family projection process* explains how insecurities in adults can be managed through shifting the focus to the next generation; the *multigenerational transmission process* describes how parents' anxieties are not transmitted equally to each child as each gets varying degrees of a parent's worry focus; *emotional cut-off* is a common way that family members use distance to reduce the sense of loss of individuality in relationships; *sibling position* was seen by Bowen as formative in an individual's relationship sensitivities; and *societal regression process* showed how the same anxious patterns in families can be seen in institutions in the broader society. All of these ideas, linked together, help show how every individual is part of a much bigger stage of actors in the same improvised play, building a storyline through their interconnections.

To see things from a systems perspective requires getting out of a 'cause and effect' way of thinking to seeing how every person's impulses are part of a circuit of reactions that flow like electric currents around relationships. It's as if relationships are a kind of dance, with each person responding intuitively to the dance steps of another. These circuits of emotional and behavioural responses in relationships shape how each individual develops. Hence getting real about ourselves in our original families requires us to get honest about how our emotional responses and behaviours flow onto others and influence how they appear to us. The good news, from a systems way of thinking, is that changing our emotional reactions and behaviours eventually flows onto changing the entire circuit of the system. That is if we can hold onto the principles that drive our change efforts in the face of others' anxiety. This is how we can make a positive difference over time, not just for ourselves but for everyone we're connected to.

Seeing the system helps to get past futile blaming

This chapter began with a caution about blaming others for our current struggles. It can't be emphasised enough how crucial this warning is if we want to be more mature and more real about ourselves. When we're finding fault with others we stop working on ourselves. Our growing gets stuck in the blame rut.

The more we can understand the generational patterns that our parents inherited, the less likely we are to falling into narrow blaming of a parent. It's not necessary to achieve universal admiration of each parent if their behaviour hasn't earned this, but we can learn to appreciate more of the context that gave rise to their particular way of managing. When our view of family members broadens beyond ascribed labels of villain, victim, saint or hero, our maturity is enhanced as we stop taking another family member's behaviour so personally. The more we can find out about the generations of our family, the more our family can be a rich resource, instead of a liability, in our growing up.

Questions for reflection

» How did I relate to each of my parents and them to me? How
  might this have influenced the way I react to others now?

» What information about each of my parents' growing up would
  help me to view them more compassionately?

» What is my common triangle position? Who did I take sides
  with in my family? Did I join with one parent as their helper in
  their difficulties with another? Was I closer to one parent and
  more distant from the other? Which two people focused on, or
  worried about, me? Did I learn to share worries and complaints
  with third parties?

part 2

MATURITY for the first half of ADULT LIFE

Leaving home and growing up
Out into the big wide world

'The person who runs away from his/her family of origin is as emotionally dependent as the one who never leaves home. They both need emotional closeness, but they are allergic to it.'[1]

— Murray Bowen MD

'Leaving home, the young person's major family transition before marriage is almost like a fingerprint, revealing the family program for handling relationship transitions.'[2]

—Betty Carter MSW

There's probably no more formative stage for growing up than the transition from being dependent on our parents to fending for ourselves away from the childhood home. The way a young person and their parents express themselves to each other during this transition reveals how much maturity has been achieved.

A healthy leaving-home transition has a reasonably good balance between connection and independence. Being able to be both an independent thinker and a caring relater is at the heart of becoming a mature adult. The young person and their parents talk openly about the plans for moving out and are able show affection and support as they express the challenges of letting go. They have each been working gradually towards more independence over a number of years. The parents' capacity to pull back from responsibility for their grown child's life, and forge a more adult relationship of mutual interest, is critical to the way a young person manages this transition.

The more mature young adult doesn't expect their parents, or others, to manage their finances for them but has worked in advance to set themselves up to manage independently. They're able to ask for help from their parents for particular setting-up-home needs and are able to tolerate listening to their parents' objections if they're not willing to assist in a particular way. Both parents and their adult child are comfortable maintaining regular contact where they share news of life but don't invite the other to solve their challenges for them. They ask each other's opinions on career and relationship issues but neither makes a project out of directing the other's life. The young person is respectful of the influence of their parents and is curious to hear stories of how they managed to leave home and be independent from their own parents.

The more mature parent is aware that the tension points that existed at the time they left home are likely to bring some anxiety to their own child's transition to adulthood. They're careful to monitor any exaggerated reactions and worries that spring out of this. The parent who is aware of what they left unresolved, when leaving their parents a generation before, can be a wonderful resource in smoothing their own child's leaving-home transition. Remembering that they struggled to be honest with one of their parents or confided too much in a parent, or couldn't wait to escape their parents' scrutiny, gives some clues about how these patterns can transfer to their relationships now that their own child is trying to make their way in the adult world. When a parent can notice their own out-of-proportion thoughts and feelings about their child leaving home they can stop themselves from focusing on their child's issues and deal with what's in their own backyard. This takes out much of the pressure in the interactions with their young adult child, who is then able to use this calmer space to also be more self-aware.

The pendulum from running away to staying dependent

The opposite ends of the leaving-home spectrum reveal the main growing-up barriers of this stage of life. At one extreme is the young person who runs or breaks away from home. At the opposite end is the young person who never manages to live without their parents' approval and support. The young adult who cuts off as quickly as possible from their parents, without being able to be an adult with them, can stay stuck in their intense anxiety about their parents being difficult. They're likely to find it difficult to be real in expressing their opinions in subsequent relationships and to distance themselves as a way of dealing with tensions.

At the other end of the pole is the young person who struggles to be separate from their parents' life. They may distance themselves for a time, when things become too intense in their relationship, but continue to be emotionally and financially interdependent. This person is more vulnerable to going through life fusing into others' lives in the same way they did with a parent. They can struggle to live life without borrowing support and validation from others.

Where were you on the continuum from dependence to running away when you left your parents' home? Have you managed to achieve more of a centre position with your parents as time has progressed?

Can you stay in regular contact with your parents and at the same time be independently responsible for yourself? Some of us will have managed to leave home and be financially independent but have never learnt to be distinct from our parents by being comfortable expressing different opinions to them. Others of us might achieve independence in parts of our life but still take on the responsibility to make a parent happy or look to them to do this for us. Their approval remains very important to us and we may edit our conversation so that we only share what will be validated.

A matter of duty or relationship building?

At the distancing end of the spectrum, we may not have run away and cut off all contact with our parents but instead keep a superficial formality to our contact. When our visits home become a matter of duty, where nothing real is shared, this reflects our use of distance to gain independence. There's hollowness in these visits home and we come to see our parents more as a burden than a resource to us. This same dance can later be repeated in our marriages and with our children.

I'm often asked in counselling sessions, 'Why would I bother having a more honest relationship with my parents after leaving home so long ago? Isn't a degree of distance appropriate to growing up and getting on with life as an adult?' To an extent these protests make sense. Some degree of distance is necessary to establish an independent life and prepare for starting a new family. The problem is that what we didn't express to our parents in an honest and responsible manner at the transition to adulthood is likely to remain unexpressed in relationships that follow. Additionally, if there were hurts and misunderstandings not worked through before leaving home, these same issues will create a heightened degree of anxiety when they appear in other relationships. If we can't be more real with our parents it will be hard to maintain authenticity in any committed or important relationship.

Larissa's story

At the age of 25, Larissa came to counselling wanting to work out a way to stand up to her father. She wanted to find a way to tell him what a disappointment he was to her, declaring that, 'This just has to happen if I'm ever going to be able to get on with my own life!'

Since her parents' divorce ten years earlier, Larissa's relationship with her dad had felt like an immense burden of obligation. At the time of her parents' separation, Larissa reported that her mother had reinvented her self-confidence with a new career and social life. She recalled that her father had fallen into a heap of despair and lost all motivation. Larissa stayed close to her mother and enjoyed a fresh connection that had been strained during the years of tension prior to the divorce. Her relationship with her father had changed, with her role becoming more that of a caretaker. She had chosen to move in with him full-time after graduating from high school so that he wouldn't be too lonely, but seven years later she was filled with resentment about his neediness. 'Even with all the support I have given him he hasn't pulled himself together to make his own friends and live a useful life.'

I asked her, 'What do you want to achieve with this proposed showdown with your father?'

Larissa replied, 'I just want to be free of having to worry about him all the time.'

I asked her if she was putting this worry responsibility on herself or was her father actually asking her to worry about him? Larissa could see that this wasn't really something her dad was asking of her. He wasn't saying to her that she must put her life energy into caring for him. Rather, it was a position she had absorbed as part of her dance with him over the years.

I then asked, 'Do you think confronting your father will help him gain a better understanding about what you are struggling to change about your life?'

After a long reflective pause, Larissa replied, 'I guess telling him how fed up I am with him will mostly hurt him. It's not going to go very far in helping him to understand my changing priorities. When I stop to think about it, I can see that venting my frustration at Dad is only going to mess things up more.'

I then asked Larissa, 'Rather than have a confrontation, what are some ways you could begin to put into action your limits in relating as a daughter, what you are and are not willing to do for him?'

Larissa was stuck for words for a moment. 'I don't think I have figured this out for myself,' she replied, 'so I certainly haven't begun to live this with Dad. I haven't really thought about what I think is a healthy job description for me as an adult daughter.'

Caring about another versus caretaking for another

As our conversation continued, Larissa realised that she couldn't keep bearing the load of responsibility for her father's emotional state and simultaneously work to be an independent adult in the world. At the same time she acknowledged that she had taken on this sense of responsibility for her father without really thinking about whether this was a healthy thing for either of them. Of course, her father had been part of the dance of the needy one and the strong one which had never been worked out in Larissa's parents' marriage.

The idea of a confrontation with her dad was clearly not going to achieve the autonomy Larissa longed for. It would only cause confusion, guilt and defensiveness through which it would be hard to find a way. Cutting off from her father was not going to be the answer either. Larissa needed to gain some understanding of how the circumstances of her family resulted in her taking on this position of feeling so responsible. She also needed to find a way to be real about how much she cared about her dad without this compulsion to take care of him. Caring about another would come to mean something very different in Larissa's life than taking care of another.

Honesty without attacking

The growing-up challenge for Larissa was to find a way to bring more honesty to her relationship, without attacking her father or trying to change him. This would involve Larissa shifting her focus from what kind of father she wished she had, to what kind of adult daughter she wanted to be. Larissa began to think through her concern for her dad and how much she wanted the opportunity to keep relating to him as an adult. Instead of telling him what she thought his faults were, she began to talk to him about how she wanted to contribute to the relationship and what she was no longer able to do. Larissa reported a conversation with her dad where she said, 'Dad, I realise I can't take on the job of improving your health, but I do really hope you can find a way to look after yourself well because I would really like to have you around for decades to come.'

Larissa wanted to share more of herself with her father instead of always worrying about him. She would say how his actions affected her relating to him rather than accusing him of behaving badly. The next time her father started reporting all his problems Larissa said, 'Dad, when you list all your problems I find myself taking them on my shoulders and I've been allowing it to drain me of energy lately. I really want to talk to you today about some of the new things

I've been doing at work and I'd like your opinion about a new job opportunity.'

Larissa decided that growing away from her father was a better option than breaking away with anger. She no longer needed to dump all her disappointments on him and could alternatively express her care alongside her honesty about her differences to her father. Additionally, she realised that she had got herself caught in the middle of her parents' marriage troubles. Her mother's relief at Larissa supporting her father after the separation had played into the confusion. Larissa had slipped into a position of over-responsibility for her dad, the way her mother had done in the marriage. She could see that she had some changes to make in her relationship with both her mother and her father.

The paradox of more family contact

At any stage of life, one of the best forums for growing up is in reconnecting with our original family and forging a more mature relationship with each family member. If we can learn to be in contact with our parents and siblings without falling back into any old ways of managing family anxiety such as distancing, blaming or rescuing, we can make some genuine progress towards maturity. Many people I have worked with have initially struggled to see the benefits of recontacting family members who seem so different to them.

I recall Anthony, a 30-year-old male telling me he was convinced that his mother was so toxic he could never have contact with her or let her track down his whereabouts. As he began to explore the bigger picture of his parents' lives and their own families, he started to tone down his negativity. When Anthony uncovered the facts of his mother's loyal friendships with others and her resilience in leaving her country of origin to get married, he could appreciate that there was more to her than the intense smothering he remembered running away from. Rather than write off his mother as impossible, Anthony started to work on his contribution to the smothering he gets into in relationships. How could he reconnect with his mother in a more balanced way? How could he hold his separateness without needing to run away? It took a lot of thoughtful planning but he did begin to make progress in having contact with his mother in a more adult way where he could listen to her and tell her about himself without thinking that she was forcing him to give her more attention. He could hear a negative remark from her and not personalise it as much as he had as a younger man.

For many people like Anthony, as they begin to take steps towards less anxious ways of relating to their parents, they discover the paradox that making more contact with family members actually helps them to separate or 'leave home' in a more constructive way.

Ongoing leaving-home issues

I frequently get requests from adult children to help them to deal with their parents, who they experience as unreasonable in their expectations or withholding of attention and support. At the same time parents, in later midlife, are asking for help in bridging the gap between them and one of their children who they feel has shut them out. The unspoken expressions of thinking and feeling from earlier years have not been resolved by the passing of time; often they become more distressing with the inclusion of in-laws and grandchildren in the complex mix of family expectations.

The keys to working through these parent–child tensions in adult life are as follows:

» Stop focusing on what we wish we could change about the other person and figure out how we might be a challenge for them.

» Work on reducing the critical intensity in our contact with the other person and check that we're not being motivated by an agenda to get them to see the world as we do.

» Check that our motivation is to bring the best of our self and our principles to our contact across the generations.

» Be willing to express points of view that may be disagreed with.

» Refrain from venting about the other person to third parties.

» Take care not to hand our parents across to our spouse, as this is a recipe for brewing misunderstandings and frustrations.

As long as we work at keeping regular personal contact with our parent or adult child, we're likely to be contributing to a more mature relationship. It might not always be a smooth and comfortable path, but it will open up opportunities to grow and gain real self-esteem and real relationships.

What about painful, unhappy families?

None of us has completely mature parents who are always consistent in their principles and behaviour. It is, however, the case that there are marked variations in what people had to deal with in terms of the challenges of family experience. For those who experienced the trauma and violation of abuse from members of their family of origin, the challenge of leaving home and defining an authentic self can be fraught with fear and anger. The principles of leaving home through forging an honest connection with parents rather than anxiously breaking away can still be helpful for many people who are carrying the pain and confusion of being mistreated by a parent. Professional guidance may well be called for in these complex situations so that there is not an escalation of anxiety that recreates unsafe experiences — but be wary of any advice that adds to the angst by advocating confrontation.

I have seen the growth in self for a good number of adults who have told their experience of abuse to family members, often with the help of carefully worked-through letters. They have been coached to communicate factually and without attack. They have also acknowledged that the abusive parent had some good qualities, which has added to their pain and sadness about the loss of trust that has come out of being abused. The effort to communicate the unspoken history of violation in a family relationship has not simply been about a one-off statement, but about an action plan to be able to walk away from any behaviour they experience as intimidating and one-sided. The longer term effort is to learn to recognise when they lose their own thinking in the pull to fuse in their family and to regain clear and safe individual boundaries. Of course, this is not a simple formula that can be applied to all difficult situations. It is a journey that each individual must think through for themself. The effort is towards defining self, not trying a relationship technique. Being clearer, in a respectful manner, with your challenging family about what principles you stand for has the potential to promote growth and reduce fear — something that blame and cut-off from family cannot achieve.

The goal is not harmony but authenticity

Reconnecting with parents and with adult children doesn't always lead to harmonious relationships. In some cases it may simply mean a more open, honest and therefore more adult relationship — even if this seems like it is only coming from one side. Whenever we take a different position in a relationship there is sure to be a counter-reaction from others to try to recreate what has become the comfortable norm. Holding onto our convictions can feel extremely hard during this predictable period of pressure to change back.

It may not be pleasurable to make contact with family members when we find their behaviour and life choices difficult to respect, but the gain in our own maturity as we move from blame to understanding can make it worth the effort. And over the long haul, the maturity effort of one person begins to ripple to other parts of the family and surprising effects sometimes emerge.

If you can achieve a steadiness in the intense emotional field of the family you grew up in, you're better prepared to express yourself maturely in the most challenging of relationship situations in other parts of your life. It's never too late to rethink how you left home. In the process of going home again with more awareness of yourself in the fabric of your family history, you may be surprised to discover a depth of friendship with family members that you never imagined was possible.

Questions for reflection

» How did I go about leaving home? Where was it on the continuum between running away and staying dependent?

» What would I need to address to have a more adult relationship with each parent:

    a) where I no longer expect them to bail me out of difficulties;

    b) where I am able to calmly discuss difficult topics;

    c) where I can be a resource to them without rescuing them or without allowing them to rescue me?

» How much have I used labels to justify avoiding being more real in my relationship with my parents (or young adult children)?

» What options for a more mature relationship open up when I focus on managing myself with my parents (or children) rather than what's wrong with them?

» What would I need to change about how I relate to my parents (or my adult child), in order to keep in line with my values and principles?

5.

The single young adult

Learning how to relate wisely to yourself

[For less mature people] 'so much life energy goes into seeking love and approval ... that there is little energy left for self-determined goal-directed activity.'[1]

—Murray Bowen MD

'Single persons have a wonderful opportunity to develop that most paramount of all relationships, the relationship with the self.'[2]

—Roberta Gilbert MD

The years after leaving the family home provide a unique opportunity to figure out how to live as an adult in the world without leaning too heavily on an intimate partner. It's all too easy to use relationships with others as a way of filling our maturity gaps. We can use a close relationship to calm us down when feeling tense and to reassure us when feeling insecure. So what's wrong with this? After all, humans are social beings who are wired for attachments. Relationships are central to creating families and communities that richly enhance the depth and meaning of life experience. The flipside to these positives is when we look to relationships to steady us, instead of taking on this responsibility ourselves. When we rely too much on relationships they can become obstacles to growing maturity.

The period of being single after leaving home can provide a vast array of opportunities to practise using inner resources to calm, reassure and provide direction, without using a relationship as a security blanket. There are many challenging transitions for the young adult in clarifying their career direction, learning to be financially independent and preparing for a life partner. Heightened anxiety about life direction is common during this phase and can present the young adult with good opportunities to learn how to keep uncertainties from being blown up into imagined fear. These anxieties about life direction can be generated in the sensitivities between a parent and their adult child. As described in the previous chapter on leaving home, the degree of family anxiety that the young adult is connected to has a profound impact on their capacity to make a smooth transition in a new phase of life. The more the young adult practises being an adult with their parents, and the parent practises relating on an adult level to their child, the more growth will be enhanced at this stage of life.

Young adults will benefit if they don't depend on external distractions such as social networking, shopping or drinking to manage their transition tensions but instead practise utilising their biological resources (such as breathing, stretching and exercising) to relax their minds and bodies. There are important opportunities to work at keeping worries under control, by using the thinking mind to examine the logic and facts of each situation. Any effort as a young adult to work on developing life priorities, principles and clarifying meaning (i.e. philosophy, faith and spirituality), will go some way to preventing big and small decision-making becoming overwhelming.

Relationships can fill maturity gaps

The temptation to fill the gaps in our maturity with a relationship can be a particular pitfall for the single young adult. As the previous chapter suggested, the young person who breaks away from their relationship with their parents is vulnerable to replacing one anxious relationship with a rushed, intense, romantic one.

Society's obsessive focus on romance can inundate the insecure, changing world of the young adult. This can put such pressure on people about being attractive to others that they compromise their development of guiding life principles. Rhonda's story illustrates how relationships can easily derail a person's growing up. At my first meeting with Rhonda she declared, 'I am over being single!' As she approached the age of 30 she thought it was time to settle down with one man and learn to be content with a slower pace in her social life. She described her twenties as a rollercoaster ride, where she had spiralled in and out of intensely passionate relationships. Each had jolted to an abrupt end, with Rhonda either discovering that her boyfriend had been two-timing or with her own eyes wandering to the next charmer who came along. Most of the men Rhonda fell for were big drinkers who loved to socialise. While she had a niggling concern about their lack of responsible behaviour, along with the irresponsible part she played in the dramas, she always convinced herself that things would change once she found the right man. Rhonda had the awareness to say, 'I know I get such a charge out of flirting. It gives me this sense of power to get men's attention. But I'm getting worried that I might never be able to get off this path of serial romances.'

Lately she had been telling herself that she wouldn't dive prematurely into a love affair but would take the time to discover the man's character. Initially she felt stronger and more adult to be able to have some boundaries with a man's attentions; but with the increase in the pace and intensity of pursuit, through text messages and phone calls, she couldn't resist jumping into another passionate fling. This was always followed by a betrayal and dramatic break-up, leaving Rhonda resigned to not fulfilling her dream of finding a soul mate. Intellectually Rhonda knew that her formula was faulty, but the intense yearning for the illusion of love was too intoxicating. She also acknowledged that there was a part of her that loved the drama of passion without the responsibilities of settling down. She was unable, at this point, to find a way to let her principles direct her feelings.

A health-enhancing relationship

It's possible to be single in legal terms yet never learn to operate as an independent adult. This was the case for Rhonda who, while not married, was rarely out of a relationship. She was still struggling in many ways to gain separate thinking space from the emotional reactivity of her original family dynamics. Her father had been a flirtatious man who had many affairs. Rhonda had joined with her mother in disapproving of her dad but had also, like her mum, longed for his attention and admired the way he could command a room with his charisma and charm. Her relationship maps were confused between the moral indignation and helplessness of her mother and the seeming popularity and power of her father's sexualised charm. She had absorbed a lot of anxiety around intimacy and was understandably confused about how to be both connected and separate in relationships.

Rhonda took a beginning step to get free of her disillusioning cycle of relationship dramas. It had all seemed insurmountable to her until she reflected on the success she had had over the past year in breaking her compulsion to binge eat. It's interesting to note that at the same time that Rhonda was turning her attention to understanding her relationship with her parents, she developed a concern about better looking after her body. Often people find more conviction to break habits when they gain a bit more of a sense of self in their families of origin. Rhonda had decided that the costs of satisfying her craving for chocolate far outweighed the immediate benefit of the calming gratification that food provided. With enormous effort she determined to break the power of this quick fix over her goal to be fit and healthy. Rhonda had actually managed to achieve it! Did this mean that if she could break the seductive power of chocolate she could follow the same path in breaking the seductive power of pseudo love? Saying no to chocolate had meant enduring the feelings of agitation and disquiet of her cravings. An even greater endurance effort would be needed if Rhonda was going to use her singleness to live with integrity, rather than sabotage her goals with serial 'quick fix' flings. This would require an effort for Rhonda to have a healthy relationship with Rhonda, as opposed to giving up her growth in the arms of a man. It took Rhonda many months of struggling with the gap between what she knew was healthy and how she felt and behaved, for her to find the conviction to begin to change. It hasn't been an easy road for her and she continues to have setbacks, but she has more compassion for her struggle to be a separate self and is determined to keep working at it.

All of us will be single at some stages of our lives, in young adulthood, or after a marriage ends in divorce, or following the death of a partner. Some will remain single throughout much of their lives. We live in a society that puts an inordinate emphasis on partnering.

In the current wave of reality TV shows a common theme is the quest of an eligible bachelor or bachelorette for a marriage partner from an array of contestants. Those who are single can be left sensing, like Rhonda, that they are somehow only half the people they could be if they could only find their soul mate.

Singleness — an opportunity to work on balance

The phase of the single young adult is ripe for laying some solid maturity foundations by working on managing independently in a variety of important life skills. As described in Chapter 2, one of the indicators of our level of maturity is the degree of responsible behaviour that we have achieved across all the important domains of life. These include managing our health and relaxation, our finances, our domestic situation, our work, our significant relationships and social relationships. Think about which of these areas you learnt to manage responsibly for yourself before you left home.

Most of us left home managing some areas well but in other areas still depending on our parents to manage for us. In my late teens I was given lots of validation for working hard and achieving good academic results but was rarely expected to clean up after myself. Hence my domestic skills have required some serious effort over the years. Maybe you did lots of nurturing and caretaking in your family and never learnt to manage your own money. Were you the person who was skilled at organising family events and remembering everyone's birthdays, but gave little attention to looking after your health and wellbeing? You might want to pause to consider these questions:

» If you're currently single, how are you working to develop your own responsible functioning versus looking to others to fill the gaps?

» If you're reading this chapter and you're married, what gaps in managing independently would be exposed if you were to become single?

» If you are a parent, are you filling in gaps for your children that might impair their ability to function for themselves one day as mature adults?

Any phase of life is a good time to consider what our gaps are in our life responsibilities. Rather than allow others to fill these in, we can choose to develop the knowledge, skill and discipline needed to be able to manage in all areas.

Lifting our discipline in these gap areas will not only ensure that singleness won't come as a major crisis for us later in life, but that our current relationships will not become unbalanced in terms of equal contributions. If you're reading this as a single young adult, now is a great opportunity to learn to stand more securely on your own two feet. This isn't easy if your family experience hasn't held you responsible for life's important tasks, but that doesn't mean that you can't begin to acknowledge your gaps and take the first steps to lift your game in these areas. It won't all come naturally and it will take a conscious effort, but the long-term benefits for wellbeing and strong relationships make it worthwhile.

Lessons on anxiety and connections with others

If being single provides opportunities to calm ourselves without the use of a relationship, it follows that we need some ideas for managing life's inevitable anxieties. Anxiety serves us well when we face a real threat that requires a quick response. Continuing to worry about imagined threats, however, is the source of many chronic symptoms for individuals and relationships.

For a short period in my early adult years I found myself worrying about developing cancer. My mother had died of breast cancer when I was 21, just before I left home. It's easy to see that my worries came from a real event, but my fears about aches, pain or unusual lumps were in my imagination. The cancer sensitivity had the potential to become a bottomless pit of worry because it was based on the fear of what might happen, not something that was actually happening. Looking back I can see that worrying about my health provided a single container where I could direct other areas of stress generated by my life changes. This didn't, however, help me to address each change in a thoughtful manner. Fortunately I was able to bring this worry down to size so that it did not create too much disruption to my life.

In the many years since, I've learnt that one of the most useful ideas for dealing with anxiety is to separate the 'what if' fears from the 'what now' worries. Practising switching off from worries that are imagined is a worthwhile growing-up skill. It's also useful to check whether you are using one worry area to take away from having to deal with a broader number of life adjustments. This might distract from lots of stressful tasks but it runs the risk of becoming an obsession that can take over our life energy. All manner of things can become anxiety binders that package lots of stresses into one thing. It could be a fear of illness or gaining weight, or something to do with sexuality or finances or cleanliness. Learning how to relate well to ourselves requires a conscious effort to spread our energy across all the aspects of life rather than turning one challenge into an all-consuming project.

Separating the 'what if' from the 'what now'

Managing anxiety healthily is an important effort at every life phase, but the single young adult suffers particular pressure from media, peers and parents to focus more on finding a partner than learning to manage stress as a single person. Hence it's worth giving some attention in this chapter to how to prevent anxiety becoming a drain on our growth.

The degree to which we live life attuned to what might go wrong in the future, especially in our relationships, has a direct link to our capacity to deal with life's challenges. If we're always on alert for threats to harmony, or carrying a fear of another being in some kind of distress, our life energy gets directed towards looking for what we're anxious about. And what happens when you start looking for the evidence of what you imagine and fear? You're sure to find confirmation for what you are looking for and then to behave as if the problem is a fact rather than imagined.

In considering parenting anxiety about a problem in a child, Bowen described the anxiety drive occurring in three stages: scanning, diagnosing and treating. These stages can describe anxiety in many phases of life including that of young adulthood. When tension arises we might start scanning our lives (or ourselves or another person) to look for evidence of what we fear; we will inevitably find possible characteristics of our fear and put a name to it; and then we begin to treat it as if it were a real problem rather than something we're afraid might occur. We can make it very hard to work out what's logical because we can put so much intellectual research into our labelling of the problem that it seems to be legitimate. Watching out for and putting a stop to going in search of what we fear is an important life management skill to learn at any stage of life.

Learning self-regulation

Anxiety can easily get directed into our relationships by overly relying on others, overly controlling others, or focusing on a distraction relationship. Relationships are great for our health if we don't let them take over our individual responsibilities; but we are vulnerable as humans to letting our relationships act as a sedative when life gets challenging. We can look to others to calm us or focus on being helpful to others to calm us down. Stress and anxiety is an unavoidable part of life and if we can learn to not fuel it with our imaginations, and learn to draw on our own body's resources to contain our stress, we become better equipped to adapt to life's challenges.

Our responses to anxiety are automatic and usually below the level of our awareness. They can impact the functioning of our entire body, including digestion, heart rate, blood pressure, adrenaline levels, breathing capacity and skin temperature. Our growing up is significantly enhanced by recognising when our relationship systems trigger internal anxiety and to recognise how our bodies express this arousal.

The more we attend to our body's stress responses and practise skills to bring down the agitation, the more choice we develop between attending to our feelings or our thinking. We can have our feelings and emotions without them having us or taking over our energies. Paying attention to our depth and pace of breathing, to our hand temperature and to our muscle tension can go hand in hand with using our mind to put anxiety triggers into logical proportion. While there are no magical techniques to managing our stress responses, we can each find strategies that make a difference for us.

A young woman's efforts to deal with anxiety overload

Twenty-five year old Sarah was struggling to understand her symptoms of burnout and fatigue. She'd been a natural caretaker in her family while growing up, picking up her mother's worry about family members being unhappy. As a nurse Sarah had found a caring profession that maintained this familiar way of relating.

When I asked Sarah how much of her energy went into reading the feelings of others, she replied: 'I spend my life looking for signs of whether others are feeling happier through my efforts! Everyone tells me I am a natural at knowing where others are at. But I've no idea what's going on for me.'

As a young single woman, this focus on caretaking and maintaining approval from others was taking its toll physically, psychologically and socially. Sarah had little energy for maintaining her friendships and was spiralling into exhausted collapse.

This near-emotional collapse had been a wake-up call for Sarah. She used it to explore new ways to manage anxiety, where her efforts went into clarifying her own opinions and views rather than trying to please others. During counselling, she made small steps of progress through learning to sometimes say no to family members' requests. She was able to explain that it was beyond her energy levels at the moment to give what was asked for. Sarah began to expand the number of friends she kept contact with, not just her needy friends. At work, as a community nurse, she pulled back in the degree of helping she offered to her patients and was surprised to notice that many of them managed better than she thought they could. She used her time alone to work on relaxation and to develop her interest in photography.

Don't be surprised by 'change back!' reactions

With her pulling back from involvement in some relationships, Sarah experienced a good deal of pressure to change back. Friends accused her of being uncaring and family members started pursuing her for more attention as they experienced her increase in personal boundaries. The pressure to change back to her old ways came both from others and from within herself as she experienced the unease of behaving differently.

She described a sense of panic as she worried about upsetting people: 'I was taken aback by how uncomfortable I felt not to be helping others all the time. Not everyone likes it either. Some of my friends are increasing their calls to tell me about their complaints and problems. It has shown me how much I have created this expectation that I'll always be there to listen.'

Sarah did manage to see that this increased pressure from friends and family was part of the temporary upheaval triggered by her behaving differently. She calmed herself with the belief that others could, in time, find other resources to manage better. Sarah knew that she would maintain a good connection with her family without needing to take on the job of being responsible for them. Her efforts were to stay as calm as possible so she could hold onto her resolve. She realised that her resilience would only grow if she learnt to tolerate the churned up emotions that came with behaving differently towards others. This was no longer the discomfort picked up from imagining what might go wrong for another; it was a new kind of anxiety that signalled progress in her growing up and learning to care for herself as an adult.

External distracters as substitutes

Most of us don't realise how little we draw on our inner resources to manage our agitations. Instead we tend to impulsively go outside of ourselves and resort to indirect distracters of the anxiety. These can become either bad habits or more serious addictions. Anxiety distracters come in almost any form, ranging from substances or food to relationship fantasies, to shopping and excessive computer use. Each distracter has varying levels of destructiveness to our, or another's, health and functioning. The main problem with external anxiety distracters is that they never take us to the issue that needs to be addressed more thoughtfully. They also prevent us from developing or paying attention to our biologically in-built tools for dealing with stress management. It's just like the child who always jumps into his parents' bed when afraid of the dark and never learns how to get his fears under control. When we don't learn how to regulate our anxieties we are more prone to getting others caught up in helping us diffuse our stress. We redirect our worry focus onto another person or allow another to take on the job of caretaking us.

Recapping on being a single young adult

There are some unique transitions for young adults as they separate from their original families, prepare for a career to financially support themselves, learn to maintain themselves emotionally and physically, and consider a long-term relationship. The way in which the family of origin has managed the leaving-home and empty-nest phase has a significant effect on the ease of the young person's transition into secure adulthood. The more a young person and their parents can stay in contact with each other while being responsible for their individual issues, the less potential for the young person to become overwhelmed by the changes they are facing.

Being single at this stage provides an opportunity for clarifying individual values and priorities with less risk of fusing into an intense relationship. A potential hurdle to growth is becoming so immersed in the intimacy of a relationship that it becomes difficult to be a distinct person. This stage is not to be misinterpreted as an opportunity for rugged individuality. Rather, it's about staying aware of being a separate, responsible self while at the same time practising relating to a variety of people. Friendships become very important to practise being distinct and connected at the same time. Learning to relate to parents and extended family in more relaxed and honest ways is valuable practice for being both independent and attached.

The effort in developing maturity in relationships for young adults and their parents is to cultivate mutual interest in the relationships. One party doesn't take on the role of worrying and advising the other, and neither looks to the other to meet their needs. The young adult will have more capacity to grow themself when they view relationships with family and friends more as a mutual exchange of life experiences rather than a process of giving and taking. Any parents who are reading this can have a crucial support role to play by working at being truly interested in your adult offspring and pulling back from advising them about how to manage in the world. The young adult, given some non-anxious space in which to draw on their own resources, will gradually learn through their own lived experience how to best support themself in the world of adulthood.

Questions for reflection

» What are the ways in which I look to others to reduce my inner uncertainties?

» How can I learn to stand more on my own two feet while staying connected to friends and family?

» What life skills could do with some extra attention?

» How can I practise using my internal calming tools to deal with stress?

» Can I see the difference between worrying about imagined things and worrying about factual problems?

» What could be changed to create more mutual interest in relationships rather than giving and/or taking?

6.

How marriage can grow people

Changing yourself and not your spouse

'In relationships with others people are free to engage in goal-directed activity, or to lose "self" in the intimacy of a close relationship.'[1]

—Murray Bowen MD

'Is anybody really ready to get married? I doubt it. Nobody's really ready for marriage. Marriage makes you ready for marriage.'[2]

—David Schnarch PhD

I can't think of any relationship that tests the strength of our inner adult as much as marriage. All our best maturity resources are required in a long-term commitment to a spouse who shares our space day in and day out. Think about the complexity of sharing decades of adult responsibilities with another person — for financial matters, for managing a home, for raising children and for maintaining connections with friends and wider family. It's a good thing that falling in love provides the necessary optimism to get us to take the plunge into such a challenging set of life negotiations with another.

When we're in the early phases of romantic love, it seems as if everything in the relationship is going our way. But just around the corner from romantic bliss is great potential to act out the worst of our inner child when things inevitably stop going our way in the daily grind of life. Think what can be triggered when the person, who we have believed will love and understand us like no other, doesn't give us what we want. Emotions can get way out of proportion to the slight that has occurred. Blaming the other takes over and, if fighting runs out of steam, distancing and avoidance of the other person takes its place. This can be followed by one spouse sacrificing their individuality for the sake of harmony in the marriage. False harmony — with one person as the gallant rescuer and the other as the fragile, rescued one — can take the place of working through the real issues of difference between us. The real-life examples that follow will help to illustrate these familiar marriage dance patterns.

The childish myths we bring to marriage

I have no idea where the time has gone but my own marriage is now moving into its fourth decade! While I still see plenty of evidence of my immaturities in my marriage, my life has been greatly benefited by the growth of a loving, respectful and intimate friendship with my husband David. It hasn't, however, all been smooth sailing, with times of strain occurring particularly upon the arrival of children. As I look back at my earlier times of dissatisfaction in the relationship there have been two consistent themes: the first is the myth that if my husband really loved me he should know what I need; the second is that I thought it was possible to improve David if he wasn't fitting into what was comfortably acceptable to me. Let's take a closer look at these two common marriage myths.

The mind-reading delusion

Expecting another person to be a mind-reader is a sign of fusion or loss of individuality in a relationship. In the early years of my marriage, I would go to bed upset about something David had or hadn't done. Unable to settle, I would toss around in bed trying to hint to him that he needed to make amends. I felt affronted to discover that he could fall into a deep sleep while I was in such turmoil! After intermittent disrupted nights, David adapted to my immature expectations of him by asking if there was anything I needed to talk to him about before his head hit the pillow. David was starting to take more responsibility for calming me down than I was taking for myself. Thankfully we have managed not to get stuck in this pattern. I have learnt to take more responsibility for calming down my own insecurities that compelled me to vent whenever I felt like it. More often I'm now able to speak clearly about what I'd like without expecting mind-reading and without attacking David for not being sensitive enough to me. I've also come to see that a good many of my early upsets were issues I could take responsibility for solving myself, such as the need for reassurance. None of this has come easily and progress has been slow and incomplete, however small efforts on yourself can make a big difference in a marriage. I have had to work to grow up from the relationship I had previously had with my mother, where she was always attuned to my emotional states and ever available to listen to me and reassure me.

The 'changing the other person' fantasy

The second myth I took into my marriage was the notion that I could change the parts of David that didn't fit my image of my perfect match. In the fanciful stage of courtship, neither of us could see any fault in the other. As the realities of living with another person came into focus, the differences that initially seemed attractive, and even cute, started to become somewhat irritating. As I became aware of David's differences, I began to focus on suggestions about how he could make adjustments. Looking back I cringe in remembering some of the feedback I would give him after dinners with friends. I would suggest how I thought he could have behaved more appropriately according to my perception of social acceptance. If he said something in a social context that I thought sounded exaggerated or uninformed, I would feel anxious and irritated.

This is a clear sign that I was seeing David as an extension of the self I wanted to portray to the world. I was looking to him to complete me as a person and one of the requirements for that was that he be socially confident and extroverted to bolster my social insecurities. It's a wonder that he tolerated such projection; but of course I now understand that we were in this pattern together. David might sometimes have been annoyed by my criticisms, disguised as guidance, but he didn't take a calm stand for himself about what he would and wouldn't put up with. Both of us were contributing equally, though differently, to the pattern of my change efforts and David's advice seeking. With David looking to me to be his mentor in many aspects of his life, I was given scope to increase my somewhat bossy over-controlling tendency. I was well programmed to slot into the advice-giving role I'd had with my mother.

Fortunately I have gradually learnt to appreciate, from lessons learnt from life and also my professional development, that efforts to change another person are counterproductive and contribute to frustration and insecurity in a relationship. I'm also aware that, when I get bogged down with the irritants I have with David, it's usually an indication that I'm not addressing an uncertainty in myself in a thoughtful way. When our anxieties get redirected into focusing on either helping or changing another, we're on a path to contributing to a much greater problem than the original issue of self-doubt or discontent.

The good news

As I take steps to shift my focus to soothing my own anxieties, addressing my own immaturity and speaking for myself in my marriage, I also allow more space for David to be his own person. He has more breathing space to make mistakes and be responsible for his own growth. This is the really good news story about systems thinking: that it only takes *one* person in a marriage to change their part in the process and the other will no longer have as much reactive fuel for their part in immature patterns. It reminds me of a tree near our first house that was spreading its large root system under one corner of the house where there was plenty of moisture. This was causing some horrid cracks to appear in the walls of our lounge room. A structural engineer suggested a way to improve the drainage around the house. With the moisture source reduced, the soil stabilised and the tree adjusted by spreading its roots more evenly. The tree was not directed to change, but it made its own necessary adjustments to fit the change in the environment. In the same way, if one person in a marriage and family identifies their contributions to an ineffective pattern, and corrects him or herself, the emotional environment changes and others independently make adjustments. Isn't this a liberating idea — to think that you don't need to try to fix things in others but simply work on what is in your control? But be prepared for slow changes in the circular patterns of relationships. Sometimes things can feel more chaotic for a while as adjustments are taking place in others. What will keep you on course is the sense of being a more responsible person, not looking for results in another.

Debunking the myths about mind-reading and changing another

person has been pivotal to my ongoing, often sluggish, but helpful, growing-up progress. In marriage, learning to recognise and speak directly about my own issues, rather than finding something to change in David, has been a step towards greater maturity. The context of a relationship, which struggles over the long haul, has provided the ideal context for me to practise learning these lessons.

The three 'maturity detours' in marriage

Just when we think we are acting in an adult manner, marriage has a way of revealing how immature we can be. Let's face it, when stress levels are increasing in our marriages, the quickest way to relieve this is to borrow from our inner child. Letting our feelings rule and focusing all our energies on the other person just seems the natural thing to do. Distancing when the heat gets too high, pushing for agreement to create a truce, or complaining to another who agrees with our view about our spouse being at fault, all serve to calm things down in a superficial way.

The central challenge in staying mature in a marriage is to find the balance between being a separate person and being a connected person. Staying separate is about managing your anxieties, addressing your own insecurities and changing the irresponsible aspects of your behaviour in your marriage. It's normal to have insecurities about whether or not you're up to new roles and responsibilities. The hard part is recognising the signs of your self-doubts and then to think through what are realistic expectations of yourself. You can then be honest with your spouse about what you're feeling and share your strategies for keeping these uncertainties from getting too big. You can welcome advice but stay in charge of thinking through what's best for you. Staying connected is about communicating with each other and acting in ways to strengthen the intimacy you committed to in choosing to get married. Efforts towards connection means efforts to refrain from avoidance and stand-offs.

The mature adult, who consciously works on being a responsible individual as well as a responsible lover and partner, is not going to be easy to attain. Remember the title of this book is directed at stopping us humans from kidding ourselves that growing up is easy. It can be extremely useful to understand the detours that can prevent you achieving a more adult marriage. Understanding what drives these common detours can give you clues about how to change your part in them. There are three maturity detours that commonly occur in marriages. Each works to relieve the anxiety generated by sensing a loss of validating connection. These are: the dance of conflict and distance, the one-up one-down manoeuvres, and doing a three-step by involving a third party. Let's look at these detours now.

The dance of conflict and distance

Do you know of couples who seem to be constantly fighting over anything and then passionately making up? The combatants often have a strangely strong connection, even though there's a lot of anger involved. Without having to work on being more responsible, each uses attack and defence to create both connection and distance. The balance of needing some space and needing to be attached is partially achieved in this dance. A 'tit for tat' kind of conflict and defence keeps the energy directed towards the other person and away from oneself. As the intensity of this focus on the other increases, the couple shuts off in anger and each gains some distance from the other.

Dianne and Julian are a clear example of this conflict-and-distance pattern. As their marriage progressed past the honeymoon phase, they found themselves arguing almost every other day. They spent many hours in heated debate about how the other was behaving badly. Accusations would fly back and forth until one of them would retreat with a huff or a slammed door. Neither was happy living their life this way but they had no idea how to get out of the cycle. What they had not appreciated was how the conflict-and-distance circuit was assisting them to deal with their needs for togetherness and separateness. The conflict created an intense, close involvement. It also reached an inevitable pressure limit from which they both retreated to the escape hatch of distance. After some time apart, they would come together with a renewed calm and ability to be passionate and loving for a short while until the next barrage of accusations began to fly.

Dianne and Julian had found a way, albeit a costly one, to balance their needs for their own space and their connection. They even described having a mutually satisfying sex life. The downside, however, was that the arguments were becoming more ferocious and the threat of moving to violent outbursts was increasing. Additionally, their daughters were growing up in an atmosphere of conflict and had begun to try to get between their parents to stop them fighting. If the marriage was going to survive, Dianne and Julian would need to find a more mature way of balancing their needs for attachment and for autonomy.

The one-up one-down manoeuvres

Have you met couples where one person seems to be strong and rational and the other appears to be fragile and reactive? You may have asked yourself how such an apparently mature person wound up married to such a childlike person. Perhaps you ask this of your own marriage. This common pattern in marriage develops gradually as one spouse becomes the expert and rescuer while the other calms themself and satisfies the other's need to feel in control by giving up their own thinking and problem-solving. One spouse feels more secure when in control; the other spouse feels steadier when their partner is less anxious.

It's a bit of a chicken-and-egg pattern, as one spouse lets the other take over, or one spouse starts taking over the other's responsibilities. Both are contributing, as one partner takes over as actively as the other gives up doing for themself. The seesaw structure of the relationship calms both spouses down in the face of potential discord. This pattern creates an illusion of a maturity imbalance, as the one-up spouse has borrowed their certainty from the one-down spouse offering their position of uncertainty. The one-up spouse has not grown their inner adult — instead they have borrowed their strength from the other's increasing weakness. Caretaking is an easy way to cover over unaddressed insecurities in much the same way that leaning on another as a prop can be.

Charles and Penny express this one-up one-down anxiety management pattern. They were often told by their friends that they complemented each other perfectly: Charles was the extrovert who always looked on the bright side, while Penny was more introverted and sensitive to what might go wrong in situations. Charles was a big-picture person who could make decisions on a whim, while Penny was focused on the details and was reluctant to move forward on any decision without exploring all possible scenarios. In the early stages of their relationship, they felt the highs of togetherness as Penny looked to Charles to help her life move forward and connect to a social network. Charles loved the feeling of being appreciated as an inspiring leader in the relationship. It was a similar position to the one he had in his family growing up, where he had become his mother's protector after his father left the family.

As the years unfolded, however, Penny began to feel less

appreciative of Charles and more dominated by him. As her feelings of suffocation started to increase she began to withdraw into a discouraged state about herself. In response Charles would increase his focus on the positive and put additional energy into cheering Penny up. Penny in turn started to take more of a one-down position in the relationship to settle the tension she was feeling with her husband. She wanted the old feelings of loving harmony to return and increasingly submitted to Charles' way of doing things as a way of creating calm. For a time, things felt better as Charles sensed Penny's appreciation for his assistance in her life, but this one-up one-down dance in the marriage began opening up some significant problems. Penny became increasingly unsure of herself and Charles started to become frustrated with her expressions of helplessness. He pulled away from what he was now seeing as Penny's negative view of the world and spent more time with his friends, whom he saw as sharing more of his positive energy. Penny was losing her admiration for Charles and started to resent the time he spent away from home. Instead of her earlier gratitude for his decisiveness she felt a growing contempt for his dominance in her life.

Both had equally contributed to this dance that began as a way of maintaining intimacy, by Penny giving up her thinking while Charles took over much of Penny's functioning. Charles appeared to be the more mature one in the marriage, but he had simply borrowed this strength from Penny as she gave up her own individuality. Penny was vulnerable to becoming quite depressed as she felt that any sense of self-direction had slipped away. Her discouragement was heightened by her teenage children beginning to complain to their father about their mum being snappy. The result of this one-up one-down pattern for Charles and Penny was a huge chasm in the relationship that had once been described as perfectly complementary.

Doing a three-step by involving a third party

You've heard the saying 'two's company but three's a crowd'. When it comes to dealing with our insecurities in our marriages, it actually goes the other way. Three becomes the comfortable number. Many tensions in marriages are calmed down by each spouse talking to someone outside the relationship who gives them support for their sense of struggle. Can you relate to the good feeling that is generated by somebody taking your side when you describe a difficulty you are having with another? In marriages there are many types of these triangle patterns that take the tension away from where it started. Triangles commonly involve a parent, a friend, a work colleague and, sometimes, when at their most intense, they take the form of an affair. Perhaps more common than any of these third parties is the triangle with one or more of the children of the marriage. Tension between the spouses can readily be reduced by one or both redirecting their energies to a child. This was the case for Joe and Samantha.

After early years of tension about in-laws, Samantha and Joe came to achieve the appearance of a calm and happy marriage through putting their focus onto their firstborn son William. Triangles had always been evident in Joe and Samantha's relationship. Conflict and insecurity had been high early on, with Samantha complaining to Joe about his lack of support for her when she felt criticised by his mother. Joe was afraid of any conflict and tried to settle tension with Samantha by distancing himself from his mother. He didn't directly address with Samantha any of his experience of moving from being important to his mother to wanting to be important to his wife. Samantha complained about her mother-in-law but did not know how to talk about her insecurity in her marriage and her lack of tolerance for not being approved of by others. Things were quite tense as Samantha pushed Joe to show his loyalty to her by standing up to his mother, and Joe felt enormous discomfort about cutting off contact with his parents. Samantha was pursuing connection by telling Joe how he should show that she was a priority ahead of his family. Joe was distancing himself from both his wife and his mother as a way of gaining some relief from his sensitivity to the pressure of each of their expectations. His cut-off from his family was the only way he knew to keep some kind of harmony in his marriage.

The release valve for all of this unspoken insecurity came when Samantha fell pregnant. All of her energies went into having a healthy pregnancy and fantasising about the kind of child she would raise. Joe was happy that Samantha didn't seem disappointed in him as her energies went into being a mother. He enjoyed this new breathing space and began to put his energy into work. Even before their son was born he had begun to fill the breach in his parents' marriage. The problem, however, was that the disconnection in the marriage had been masked rather than tackled. The intense emotions had now escaped from one relationship, ready to be invested in a child. While William might have been the recipient of plenty of attention, the intensity of this focus would be likely to overcrowd his necessary breathing space to grow as an individual.

How to interrupt your part in the detour dance

Which of these patterns can you identify in your marriage or in your parents' marriage? For most households, one of these patterns predominates. The patterns may vary in their intensity and may not result in a major problem. Each relationship exchange can make it easier for us to cover over our immaturities in getting our togetherness and separateness needs met, but this will be at the expense of the growth in maturity of one or more members of our family.

What's the alternative to each of these detours? For each of the couples described, the growing-up formula is the same. Dianne and Julian, Penny and Charles, and Joe and Samantha all need to take their focus off the tensions of the relationship and focus more on what's happening within themselves. There may be many layers to peel back to see what hasn't been dealt with in yourself but the shift in focus from what's wrong in the other to what can be changed about yourself is the starting point to a healthier marriage. The focus on self is needed to be able to stay a separate, responsible person in the marriage. From a more solid position you will be free to connect by sharing what you think and feel and accepting each other's unique ways of behaving. Remember that it only takes one spouse to work on themself for the detour pattern to be interrupted.

Breaking the conflict cycle

Dianne or Julian would need to learn to get the focus off what they thought was wrong with the other, seeing that this effort wasn't constructive. They would need to speak their own experience without attacking the other or going on the defensive. It might sound a bit of a stretch for Dianne and Julian, but here is an example of how more direct, person-to-person communication, could occur: Julian comes home from work to an exhausted Dianne. She greets him saying, 'I'm glad you're finally home so you can help out around here!'

Rather than move into his customary defence of saying what a hard day he's had, Julian says, 'I'm really drained from my day and not up to pitching in and helping until I've had a bit of time to catch my breath.'

Dianne responds with increased annoyance saying, 'You always think you're the only one who's had a hard day. Do you have any idea what I've been up against with the kids' routine and the never-ending list of errands?'

Julian takes a deep breath and decides to refrain from taking the old conflict bait. He calmly says to Dianne, 'After a bit of time out, I'm willing to take over the kitchen clean-up and do my bit with the kids so that we can get some time to catch up on each other's day.'

Dianne responds cautiously, saying, 'Okay Julian, I'll accept that, but I need to know how long it'll be before you can help me out.'

With Julian able to draw on his inner adult to hold back from the usual defensive position, he changes the direction of his and Dianne's predictable end-of-day dance. Dianne, in response, starts to calm down a little and speak her position. They have stopped criticising each other and have opened the way to being able to work together to get the children to bed and spend some pleasant time catching up with each other.

Evening up each spouse's responsibility

For Penny and Charles to interrupt the pattern of one-up and one-down in their marriage, one or both would need to look at what contribution they are making to this imbalance. Charles would need to pull back from problem-solving for Penny and start to create space in which to really listen to her ideas. Penny would need to look at how withdrawing into quiet resentment does nothing to help her be more of a solid person with Charles. Neither will find this a comfortable process as each has learnt to either take over from others or give over to others in the families they've grown up in.

Shifting the focus off the child

Joe and Samantha would need to get in contact with each other more regularly and not just talk about how their son is doing. They would endeavour to have more of a person-to-person relationship, where each shares their own joys and struggles without expecting the other to fix things for them. This is central to establishing a connection that doesn't become overwhelmed with intensity.

Joe would improve the marriage if he worked out what kind of relationship with his mother would fit his values. He would need to reconnect with his mother and his wife without falling into the trap of trying to earn their approval. What a maturity challenge this will be for him! Samantha can strengthen the marriage by allowing Joe the space to relate to William without her interference or correction. Creating the space for Joe and Samantha to each have a separate relationship with their son is a step towards dismantling the triangle. The most important step for Joe and Samantha in getting out of this triangle is to keep their own problems within their relationship. This means being direct with each other about what isn't working for them and learning to stay in contact, even when it feels uncomfortable. The directness is not about what the other is doing wrong but about what Joe and Samantha think and feel and how they will back this up in their actions.

The growing-up paradox of marriage

Most people come to couples counselling saying they're here to work on their relationship. The irony is that the couples who make progress are the ones who stop focusing on the marriage itself and start directing their attention towards their own behaviours.

This is the paradox of growth within a marriage: that a responsible focus on yourself, and not the relationship, can bring the utmost degree of mutual satisfaction. If you want a better marriage, you will need to give up making a project out of changing the relationship or your partner and instead make a project out of expressing your own maturity within it. If you look to relationships as a path to fulfilment, through being affirmed by another person, you're likely to wind up being disappointed. To be grown up in a marriage is to see the relationship as a place to express yourself honestly and to give up expecting that your spouse be responsible for making you feel good. This effort will, over time, lead to being more accepting of each other's strengths and vulnerabilities and enjoying the intimacy of two people growing up alongside each other.

Questions for reflection

» What unrealistic expectations of your spouse have you brought to your marriage?

» Which of the three maturity detours are you most prone to:

    a) conflict and distance;

    b) over- and under-functioning;

    c) focusing on a child or third party?

» What could you pay more attention to in order to be a more mature self in your marriage?

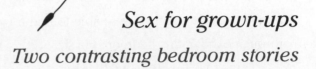

7.

Sex for grown-ups

Two contrasting bedroom stories

'Man [and woman] needs human closeness but is allergic to too much of it.'[1]

—Murray Bowen MD

'Profoundly meaningful sex is determined more by personal maturation than physiological reflex.'[2]

—David Schnarch PhD

Peter and Josie have only had sex on two occasions during the past year. Peter doesn't complain because he says he has no right to ask for sex if Josie isn't going to enjoy it. Josie says that she has never enjoyed sex and blames much of this on her mother telling her that sex with her father had always felt like rape — a powerful message to carry from one generation to the next! Both Josie and Peter were disappointed with the direction their fourteen-year-long marriage and love life had taken. Josie was carrying a big store of resentment that Peter had not turned out to be the man she'd hoped for. Peter desperately missed sexual intimacy but he never discussed this because of his nervousness at confronting Josie's dislike of him. It felt safer for Peter to continue along the path of avoidance.

In contrast to Josie and Peter, Cheryl and Hugh had always had an intensely passionate, adventurous sex life. Their marriage was in its eighteenth year with two teenage children but this hadn't in any way dampened their frequency of passionate lovemaking. Even after a raging argument, they were able to find a way back to each other through exhilarating bedroom physicality.

You may well be thinking that this couple have got it made, with such a lively sex life after having two children! Beneath the passionate surface, however, was a story of infidelity and a resulting huge chasm in emotional intimacy. Cheryl and Hugh had always agreed to an open arrangement in their marriage, which emerged from their days in the hippie culture of the 1970s. They regularly attended swingers' parties believing that such freedom strengthened their marriage; but this ideal was shattered when Cheryl started to see more of one of the party attendees. This affair with a married friend of theirs was developing an emotional intensity that threatened the future of their relationship. While they believed that there was no shortage of passion in their marriage, Cheryl and Hugh had become like strangers to each other. Their interests seemed to have diverged and they had lost the will and confidence to connect in their conversations.

Different stories, similar problems

It may surprise you that these apparently very different stories, which emerged in counselling sessions, actually reflect very similar problems. Both couples had not learnt what's required to have mature intimacy in both their relationship and their love life. Peter and Josie were avoiding their disappointments and the potential of failing in their lovemaking as their way of preserving some remnant of peace. Hugh and Cheryl were using regular sex to bypass working out their differences and staying connected as individuals. Both couples were avoiding addressing uncomfortable issues.

Both Hugh and Cheryl acknowledged that they regularly fantasised about being with other partners while having sex. This was enabling them to avoid the tension of being truly present with each other. Just like Peter and Josie, they had not developed a way to be consistently open with each other about their yearnings, insecurities and disagreements.

The grown-up challenge

Sex has perhaps more potential than any other part of a relationship to bring out our anxieties about closeness and distance. There's so much childhood neediness about being loved and accepted that gets wrapped up in having sex. The merging of our bodies that happens when we make love can all too easily take us back to a place like a suckling infant, where nurturing is on tap. Immature sex happens when lovemaking becomes a one-way street, designed to meet our needs for pleasure, attention and approval. The enjoyment of this bodily merging can be terrific, but it can also become fraught with tension if we don't remember to be separate people, expressing this separateness to each other.

Just as the previous chapter on marriage emphasised, the grown-up challenge is to bring yourself to the relationship instead of focusing on what the other can do for you. This will mean tolerating the discomfort of your insecurities with sex as much as bringing your initiative to lovemaking. It will mean not taking the other's response personally but allowing them to be a separate person who is often not going to be in exactly the same place as you in terms of sexual energy.

The potential for using sex to gain validation from another is high and is fed by a culture that uses sex to sell just about everything, from chocolate to swimming pools. When we lose our boundaries in sex, through too much other-focused sensitivity, we can easily become overwhelmed by uncomfortable closeness. That's where the detour of distancing comes in. We might distance physically like Peter and Josie. Or distance emotionally like Hugh and Cheryl, who could have electric sex but take their minds to a far removed place. In their separate fantasy realms neither was actually present during sex.

Casual sex, or fantasy pornographic sex, can easily become a receptacle for tensions that have escaped from other anxious relationship experiences. It can give an illusion of intimacy without us needing to be really known in the relationship. Once there is commitment in a relationship and two people have to bump up against each other daily, sex can no longer be a place to hide from ourselves. While sex in marriage can certainly be a place for grown-ups to play together, this is very different from being a place to escape from being real.

Bringing the inner adult to the bedroom

Hugh and Cheryl made a genuine effort to figure out what had gone wrong in their relationship but they eventually ended up going their separate ways. Cheryl decided that she had gone too far down the track of investing in her affair to be able to work at repairing things with Hugh. Both could see that they had each contributed to their growing apart and were able to separate without the common bitterness that emerges with an affair.

Things took a different course for Peter and Josie, who were able to make solid progress in bringing mature sex into their marriage. The first step to bringing more of their inner adult to their bedroom was to understand their patterns of relating from the families in which they grew up.

Peter appreciated the influence of coming from a family that avoided conflict at all costs. He saw how he was living out this script in more than just his sex life. At work his confidence was high due to regular validation from work colleagues, but at home he was becoming increasingly compliant in order to preserve peace with Josie.

Peter began to see clearly what was getting him in a hole in his marriage. He reflected:

> I'm starting to get it now. The more I'm going along with everything to avoid Josie's criticisms, the less energy I'm putting into my responsibilities at home. I can see how much I've stopped following through on things I agree to do for the children. I'm also really slacking off with the household finances. It's not something I'm doing deliberately, it's just evolved this way; and it's just too easy to let Josie take over.

Josie was carrying her mother's negative message about sex into her own marriage but she could see that this was not the single contributor to her withdrawal from sex. Josie described her initial attraction to Peter:

> I just loved what a gentle man he was. He never got angry the way my dad used to lose it. I spent so much of my teenage years listening to my mum's complaints and being angry with my father for not making her happy. When Peter came along I saw him as my 'knight in shining armour' who was going to be everything my father wasn't.

As the eldest in her family, Josie had been the responsible one who did things for others. Not surprisingly, she found herself doing more than her share in her marriage in terms of domestic tasks, parenting, bill paying, organising socialising and keeping contact with both her family and Peter's. This was on top of working part-time. Early in her marriage to Peter, she had enjoyed the closeness of lovemaking, although she found it difficult to relax and experience orgasm. As the years progressed and Josie became burdened by how much she was carrying for Peter and the children, her resentment for Peter grew. Rather than thinking through how much of a load was reasonable for her to take on, Josie put increased effort into changing Peter by giving advice and delegating tasks in a nagging tone. Peter would agree to do things, motivated by his desire to keep the peace rather than making a considered choice. As a result of his lack of ownership of the tasks, Peter would often forget or avoid his commitments. Josie's underlying contempt and Peter's sense of inadequacy was on the rise. As they uncovered these patterns they each declared that it was no wonder there was such an impasse in the bedroom!

Getting beyond blame and just doing it

When I first met Josie and Peter they each stated how committed they were to holding onto their marriage. This conviction assisted them to work hard on understanding themselves, even though they felt disillusioned about their relationship. They got beyond blaming themself or each other, and understanding how their 'seesaw' pattern, of Josie being one-up and Peter operating in the one-down position, was preventing a genuine intimacy. At the same time as addressing their contribution to these imbalances, Josie spoke of her wish to break the pattern of her sexual avoidance. To take some of the intensity out of resuming sex, she decided to put some dates in the calendar for their lovemaking. Peter expressed that he was up for this. They liked the motto of 'just do it' to address their habitual avoidance. Josie stepped forward to take the lead to reverse the distancing and get back some sexual intimacy. She wasn't focused on sex needing to be great to begin with; she just wanted to push through her anxious avoidance. Josie reported:

> I'm still not relaxed about sex and about being so vulnerable with Peter. I have to work really hard to turn off the negative thinking when we start to get close. What keeps me hanging in there is remembering that I want my marriage to work and I don't want a marriage without passion. The funny thing is that I do actually end up enjoying sex and have an increased feeling of being close to Peter. It lasts for a few days and really helps to lower my critical attitude with him.

It was not a complete, easy fix for Peter and Josie in restoring their love life and changing old patterns, but they were quick to begin taking action on their goal to improve things. Each could see that they wouldn't get to first base if they kept anxiously focusing on the other. Josie worked to focus on her choice to be sensual in her marriage rather than focus on her disappointments with Peter. Peter struggled to get the focus away from monitoring Josie for the signs of her disappointment in him.

The progress they reported over the coming months wasn't tied up in any sexual techniques or in the intensity of their orgasms. Things were improving because of their efforts to rise above their self-doubts and to push themselves to give the best that they could each muster of themselves, both in and out of the bedroom. Josie and Peter's story once again illustrates the paradox of mature intimacy; that when the focus is taken away from the relationship and placed on being a responsible, distinctive self, the greater the options for deep togetherness.

Pushing through the anxiety of making progress

Are you getting the picture of what personal maturity looks like in a sexual relationship? Grown-up sex in a committed marriage may take time to develop. It will require you to pass through times of raw vulnerability without needing to retreat or expecting your spouse to absorb your insecurities. I hope you can hear a familiar theme in this message: that growing up requires tolerating discomfort without needing a relationship to take the tension away. It's like the experience of a child who walks to school without their mother for the first time. The tension will be high and can easily be relieved by running back home, but the sense of achievement gained by dealing with the anxiety and continuing on to school is what assists the child to grow.

When sexual expression is based on personal maturity, instead of the absence of wrinkles and cellulite, it's possible to enjoy all of its erotic pleasures while staying sensually present with each other. Our society has made such a big deal of sex as being at the centre of life's excitements that many of us are confused about what to expect of ourselves and our partners sexually. Taking the intense expectations out of sex and accepting that it is basically instinctual, could go some way to reducing the anxiety that gets in the way of much sexual intimacy.

The lifetime commitment of marriage takes the urgency out of needing to work out how to be completely sexually comfortable overnight. When you manage to lift yourself out of boundary blurring in your marriage, you have more ability to choose what you focus on. You can be free to be independent in your goal-directed activities and free to choose to jump into the delicious immersion of 'one flesh' sexual intimacy. You can stop looking for personal gratification from your lover and as a result you can choose to let go of any anxious defences and allow your natural instincts of pleasurable attachment to take over.

Sex is no different to any other growing-up challenge in that it provides an opportunity to tolerate the discomfort of becoming more separate while in real contact with an important other. It can also be a joyous celebration of what it means to be comfortable in one's own imperfect skin with another imperfect but deeply known mate.

Questions for reflection

» What are the ways I tend to avoid my insecurities in my sexual relationship? Do I tend to use physical withholding or fantasy avoidance?

» How do I bring issues of approval and disapproval (do you approve of me, do I approve of you?) into my sexual relationship?

» How can I have realistic expectations of sex for two human beings who each have strengths and vulnerabilities?

» What are some ways I can practise tolerating discomfort during intimacy with my spouse rather than retreating to a tension-free zone?

8.

Grown-up parenting

Setting an example for the next generation

'The child functions in reaction to the parents instead of being responsible for him/herself. If parents shift their focus off the child and become more responsible for their own actions, the child will automatically — perhaps after testing whether the parents really mean it — assume more responsibility for him/herself.'[1]

—Michael Kerr MD

'Parents are the hope of civilization. Much depends on whether parents can connect in a meaningful, positive way with each other and with their children. If they can, a generation may emerge ready to tackle and reverse some ominous trends.'[2]

—Roberta Gilbert MD

If marriage is one of the most challenging growing-up relationships we will encounter, parenting is the place where our marriage tensions can be most disruptive. We can unknowingly use our children to redirect our own uncertainties, unaddressed resentments and unrealised aspirations. To be a grown-up parent, the task will be to get these adult issues out of the way of how we relate to our kids. This isn't at all easy to do, as these detours tend to happen without our awareness. This task of being a grown-up parent is perhaps more difficult to achieve than ever. In our current anxious, child-focused society it requires a parent to swim against the emotional tide. We will need to shift our focus away from doing for and worrying about our child and back to being a responsible self. Sound familiar?

Today's parenting: swimming in a sea of anxiety

Around my neighbourhood the worst of the morning peak hour is at school drop-off time. Frazzled parents are chauffeuring their children to school with minutes to spare before class begins. They are checking to see that their child has all their homework and correct books for the day's lessons. Children are delivered to the school gate carrying gym bags, musical instruments and laptops for extracurricular activities. The sight of groups of children walking or riding bikes to school has become a novelty. What is going on here?

It seems that the more frantic the pace of life becomes, and the more anxiety mounts about our uncertain future, the more society panders to its children. There is less space for children to think and solve problems for themselves, as both parents and schools manage their schedules for them. While the statistics tell us that those who abuse children are usually within the family or known by the family, the anxiety about 'stranger danger' and the risks of leaving a child unaccompanied by an adult have contributed to the demise of children finding their own way to school. Parents are increasingly taking over their children's homework assignments so that they don't fall behind in an increasingly results-driven climate. When a child stumbles at school, parents move in to complain to the school about not protecting their child. The school recommends a range of professional interventions to prevent the child from struggling. Meanwhile many children are less able to take a stand for themselves against schoolyard teasing; they are less able to direct their own learning efforts; and when adolescence arrives, they are ill prepared for managing their new freedoms responsibly.

The sea of ever-changing advice coming from child psychology has not always helped parents who want to do their best for their child. Peter Stearns, a professor of social history at George Mason University, Washington DC, has studied trends in US parenting over the last century. He notes that as parenting manuals emerged in the twentieth century they became a stimulus and outlet for parents' worries and added fuel to a 'century of anxiety about the child and about parents' own adequacy'.[3] As parents outsource their development of child-rearing wisdom they can easily become more uncertain in themselves.

Can you see the parenting challenge in the midst of this rush to take over children's capacities to soothe their upsets and solve their problems? If you're going to assist your child to grow their resilience, the first step will be to increase your own resilience in tolerating your child's upset without feeling compelled to rush in and smooth over everything for them. The grown-up parent, who really wants to be a loving resource to their child, is prepared to work on themselves and not make a project out of their child.

Helping children through your own maturity

Ed and Linda relished the prospect of starting a family as soon as they had established some degree of financial security. For many of their early years of marriage they enjoyed imagining the large family they would have. They spoke of how their children would enjoy the huge stores of affection that both felt they had to give.

Linda viewed her own parents as cold and distant. She was the eldest of two daughters and was distressed to recall the struggles her younger sister Rebecca experienced with depression and school difficulties. Her mother, with her dad's support, had channelled much of her energy into getting help for Rebecca. Despite her parents' efforts, Linda believed that the lack of affection in her family was to blame for her sister's struggles. She was determined to reverse this in her own family by being always available to her children and showering them with praise and warmth.

Ed was supportive of this approach. He had come from a family where his father used alcohol to switch off after work and the rest of the family walked on eggshells around him, trying to avoid an angry outburst. Ed was pleased to have found a woman like Linda who was going to be such a good mother. He was anxious about his fathering and was secure in the belief that Linda was going to lead the way in creating the happy family they both dreamed of.

After giving birth to three children within five years, Linda and Ed were feeling exhausted from chronic sleep deprivation and the energy being invested in their children. Ed was showing signs of severe burnout and was fearful that he could no longer maintain proficiency in his job as a teacher. Linda was supportive of his efforts to get some help for his symptoms so that they could keep things afloat.

It was at this point that I came to hear of this family's story. Ed came to counselling wanting to address his levels of anxiety and exhaustion. I recall him saying, 'I have only ever wanted to be a good father and a good provider; but the way I'm feeling lately I am not much use to anyone. I actually would just like to be able to run off to a retreat somewhere and not be responsible for anything.'

As Ed reflected on his fathering, he could see that he was consumed with affirming his children and guiding them well. He was crushed by his growing impatience with his eldest child. He feared that he was becoming an angry, disengaged parent just like his experience of his own father. He and Linda had read just about every parenting book available but were finding that the more they read the more confused they were becoming. They found themselves trying all manner of techniques to manage the increasingly anxious behaviour of Harry, their seven-year-old son, and their five-year-old daughter Shari's defiance. In any one day Ed found himself using time out, spanking, removal of TV, lying down with his kids to help them sleep and giving sticker rewards for good behaviour. The anxieties of their eldest son Harry had started to emerge at school and the teachers were concerned about his slow progress with reading. Ed felt that Harry was frightened to make any mistakes at school.

When I met with Ed and Linda together I heard that she also was feeling overwhelmed and directionless as a parent. Linda said, 'I have worked so hard to be up on all the latest parenting techniques and child development knowledge. You can't imagine how deflated I am that two of my children are not settled and happy.'

Overly focusing on having happy children

In turning to outside professional sources, Linda and Ed were desperate to be perfect parents for their children. The problem with this emphasis on what the books and courses said should happen was that Linda and Ed were borrowing their wisdom from others. In the process they stopped developing their inner adult, who thinks through dilemmas for themselves before rushing to get an expert's opinion. The other problem of focusing on the 'how to' of parenting is losing a focus on growing oneself. Mature parenting is not related to good technique but to nurturing a parent's character. I remember Ed's comments when he started to realise this: 'Wow,

I'd not really ever stopped to notice how much of my energy has been going into trying to have healthy and happy children. I haven't given myself much of a look-in. I guess it's not any wonder that I've fallen in such a heap.'

Ed began to see that in trying to get his children to be a certain way, he was neglecting clarifying and managing how he wanted to be as a husband and father. In beginning to redirect his focus away from the children and onto his management of himself, Ed began to pay attention to how often he tried to push, pull or praise his children. He practised pulling back and thinking through how he could manage his own emotions and then to let his children know what he stood for. This meant he got clearer about what he was willing to do for his kids and what he expected them to learn to do for themselves. As with any growing-up effort, the valuable progress comes gradually but Ed could quite quickly see the benefits of turning his attention from his children to managing himself better.

Linda was also encouraged by Ed's improved clarity and started to get interested in re-focusing her worries from her children to herself. As a result, they both started to talk more to each other about themselves, their experiences, their challenges and what they were each encouraged by in all parts of their life. As a couple they began to talk less about how to help the children and more about their values as parents and what kind of balance each wanted to get back into their lives. They also started to be more of a fun couple again. Their sense of humour seemed to have been left behind at the very thought of pregnancy.

Being clearer about expectations

Ed reported on the growing-up progress he was making, giving an example of how he managed himself at a recent school meeting about Harry. He and Linda were meeting with Harry's teacher about her concerns that he might have a learning delay. Ed reflected:

> I was able to listen to the teacher's concerns and ask her questions. But for the first time, I was able to think for myself about Harry and give my different point of view. I said that I would be okay about reviewing things at the end of the year, but I saw that a big part of Harry's problems were tied up in him being too anxious about everyone's expectations. I really stood by my new commitment to taking all this pressure off Harry.

Ed went on to say that when the teacher suggested an intensive reading course for Harry, he was clear in expressing his newly clarified view that what Harry needed most was to have some more breathing space to find his own learning potential. Linda was less certain about this approach but willing to give it a go. The teacher said she was concerned but would be happy to see how things went over the next term.

Ed's changed interactions went like this:

Harry: 'Dad, I can't do this reading! Can you come and read me a story?'

Ed: 'Harry, I am not going to come to your room until I've finished helping Mum clean up. When I come I am willing to share the reading of your school book that you've been working on.'

Harry starts whinging: 'Mum, Dad won't read me a story. Dad, you are being mean!'

Ed replies calmly and firmly: 'I have nothing more to say, Harry. I'll be in to join in your reading when I'm ready.'

Ed and Linda did not respond to Harry's protests. When Ed went to his son's bedroom at his usual time, he said: 'Show me where you're up to Harry and I will read the next three pages with you, taking it in turns.'

Ed didn't check up on how much practice Harry had done, he simply joined in reading a paragraph at a time. He didn't over-praise Harry's efforts but asked him what he liked about the story and to share his favourite character.

Ed was really motivated to change his old ways of behaving. This came from his clarity that his old approach wasn't working for his child or for his functioning as a healthy adult in the world. He determined to stop looking to the latest parenting fad for advice and began to turn his attention to his own self-management. He also began to work on bridging the distant relationship he had with his ageing parents and getting out more just with Linda. Ed also knew he would have to tolerate Harry's clinging and that his apparently helpless behaviour may continue to invite him back into doing too much for him again. He had seen enough early encouraging signs that, when left to his own devices, Harry could achieve more than he had imagined was possible.

Grown-up parents help grow up children

I can relate to the path on which Ed and Linda found themselves. When I first became a parent I recall feeling enormous pressure to get it right and not damage my children. I also felt niggling uncertainties about whether I was up to this job. Many parents, to varying degrees, struggle to get balanced about the amount of attention they give their children. With all the best intentions, we conscientious parents have a tendency to shift our focus from our own responsibilities to attending to our children's happiness.

Here's a nutshell description of what can happen with an increase in worry focus directed towards a child. See if you can follow this common cycle for conscientious, caring parents:

» In response to a parent's concerned attentions, the child becomes attuned to being nervously monitored and reacts with increasing self-consciousness.

» The child's anxious response can be in the form of increased neediness or agitated behaviour. An aroused child usually increases their impulsive and demanding behaviour, while a needy child increases their dependence.

» The parents, in turn, may inadvertently increase their focus on fixing things for the child by either increasing their corrections or their support. In this concern-driven cycle, the parent partly gives up being a separate person from the child and the child grows up borrowing some of their self from the reactions they elicit from their parent.

» The aroused child is restricted in their capacity to find ways to calm themself and contain their impulsiveness; and the needy child is compromised in learning to manage their own worries.

When a child's behaviour is anxious or unsettled it gets tricky to see the bigger picture of the parent–child circular dance. It's all too easy to think that the problem is in the child who is, after all, showing symptoms. On the other hand, the parent can be blamed for being too lenient or too harsh. What is harder to see is that the problem is mostly being generated by the reactions between people, not simply from within one individual. Both parents and children are triggering certain behaviours in the other. For example, when a child is whinging and clingy, it's all too easy to see the problem residing in the individual rather than in the system of interactions. The grown-up challenge is for the parent to look at how their efforts to assist the child may be stirring up an increase in the child's anxiety-driven reactions.

When parents start getting over-involved in either negative or positive ways with their children, this is often an overflow of tension from another relationship. Tensions that have not been figured out with parents or spouses get so easily redirected into trying to make everything work for the next generation. In the process we adults stop being direct with each other about our own concerns and insecurities and one of our children can step into the connection gaps that have been unknowingly left open for them.

Children so easily fill a breach in their parents' marriage. The solution is to be found in one or both parents shifting their focus off their child and back onto their own issues and responsibilities. Responsible, mature parents, with clear inner convictions, will in turn allow more scope for the development of responsible self-directed children.

A healthy connection with your children

You may be thinking that all this emphasis on getting the focus away from our children and back onto our own responsibilities ignores the important relationship bond that is required for a child to grow up securely. Attachment between parent and child is wired into our biology and even begins in the uterus as a foetus is able to discriminate its mother's voice from the voices of others. The challenge of healthy attachment with our children is to keep our attentiveness in proportion. The worst forms of neglect and rejection of children grow out of an idealised parent–child bond where the first signs of lack of compliance by the child are experienced by the parent as an intolerable threat to the perfect harmony they imagined. An over-idealised bond with a child can conversely take the form of too much smothering, where the child is slowed from developing as a separate person.

The following list compares the qualities of *a healthy, mature connection* with your children with an *out-of-proportion connection*, which in Bowen's theory is also referred to as fusion.

Healthy, mature connection

When part of a healthy and mature connection with our children, each person:

» enjoys both time together and time apart;
» treats each other with warmth and respect;
» displays acts of kindness and affection;
» tolerates the other being upset with them;
» is able to have disagreements without breaking the relationship;
» takes responsibility for their actions;
» responds thoughtfully.

Out-of-proportion connection

Conversely, in an exaggerated connection, or fusion, each person may:

» feel uncomfortable with separation;
» need the other to be happy with them all the time;
» expect the other to make them feel good;
» stay silent on their view because of fear of conflict;
» mind-read or speak for the other;
» think more about the relationship than their own responsibilities;
» respond anxiously.

The shift from a stifling connection to a balanced connection can bring marked changes to the parent–child relationship — indeed to all relationships. A mother of a fifteen-year-old recently described this change:

Before I started to work on my own limits with Sophie, she was shifting from awful defiance to childlike clinging to me. She was escaping out of her bedroom window most nights to hang out with friends and the next minute she'd be sitting on top of me wanting me to hug her like a baby. This was really doing my head in with her both rebelling and clinging like crazy. But over the past few months, as I have become a clearer parent, she's treating me with more respect. I'm no longer stopping what I'm doing to give her a hug but we are going for coffee together and she's talking more than I can remember. I cancelled her mobile phone connection last week and she stopped talking to me for a couple of days, but yesterday she was telling me all about her textile assignment and asking me about my day. I can actually see that we could become friends as the adult years get closer.

How parenting revealed my own immaturity

After four years of marriage, my husband David and I excitedly welcomed our first child, Jacqueline. She was the first grandchild, which meant a significant new chapter for every member of the extended family. It is not surprising that Jacqueline, like other eldest children and first grandchildren, has grown up under a spotlight. It's not easy for such children to learn to tolerate being part of a crowd without standing out.

We doted on our daughter and relished the attention she received from the wider family. As Jacqueline showed signs of evening colic, I struggled to settle her to sleep at night and became anxious about the detrimental effect of a baby crying for extended periods with her parents unable to soothe her. Like many first-time parents, I feared that she might be somehow scarred for life.

I admit I was completely unprepared for the extent of the changes that came with becoming a parent. My marriage had felt solid during the pregnancy but the job of raising a child meant lots of new things had to be negotiated. How were we going to share the load of caring for our child, dealing with domestic order and a change in our financial circumstances? No advice could adequately have prepared me for the sleep deprivation and increase in demands that I felt. Time to just chill out as a married couple had been suctioned away by the intensity of our new roles.

Rather than recognise and soothe my own anxieties about my transition to parenting, I readily focused on Jacqueline. This detouring of my uncertainties meant that I became sensitive to any sign of insecurity in Jacqueline. I responded with doting attention and stimulation. Not surprisingly, Jacqueline did develop quite distressing tantrums around age three and displayed significant jealousy of her sister Katie when she was born. This was demonstrated through aggressive behaviour such as pushing her baby sister's head into the ground and an episode of using her new safety scissors to give her sister a 'back to the scalp' haircut. While the punk hairstyle episode is retold two decades later with much humour, I can now look back and understand that it was more than quaint playfulness. My intense investment in my first child was not helping her to be able to tolerate sharing my attention with her sister.

David and I stumbled our way through the maze of early family life with times of joyfulness intertwined with chaos. My focus on giving our children the attention I thought they required, and seeking to meet what I perceived to be the expectations of doting grandparents, meant that my 'inner adult' got a bit lost. In order to grow up in this stage of my life I needed to step back from the focus on keeping children and extended family pleased in order to get my individual act together.

Rewards and punishments: lessons from puppy management

Whenever I present a talk on parenting, I am inevitably asked the question: 'Can you tell me how to get my child to do what I tell them to do?' The quest to find effective discipline techniques for children of all ages has a lot of followers. It's easy to recognise ineffective discipline: emotions out of control, impulsive slapping and exaggerated threats that will never be followed through.

The general wisdom on calm, effective parenting includes many familiar techniques for discipline such as time out, ignoring undesirable behaviour and removing privileges. Well-known techniques for reinforcing desirable behaviour include praise, granting extra privileges, and rewards such as presents and star charts. In many ways all of these approaches can be sound strategies that can bring about positive behaviour change in children and adolescents. But I wonder if you can see what is missing from all of them?

Behavioural approaches to parenting are all focused on influencing the conduct of the child rather than on the emotional regulation of the parent. While parenting our child is very different to managing our pets, I've been able to see some parenting principles illustrated as I watch how I operate with my one-year-old cocker spaniel puppy Hendrix. Food is a wonderful motivator for him to perform submissive behaviours by responding to commands such as 'sit', 'down', 'stay' and 'come'. I can even get Hendrix to drop his ball for me to throw, if I have a treat to give him. The problem is that he now has the idea that he is in charge of me as I hand food over to him and praise him for taking it. I realise that my focus on punishments and rewards is not helping me to earn his respect as the pack leader. The more useful approach with my puppy is for me to convey calm and strong leadership energy and refuse to move forward with an activity until the dog is in a submissive, non-aroused state. In this approach all the work is on myself as the owner and not directed at the dog. The dog senses when the owner is taking charge and not tolerating anxious, dominant behaviour.

Of course, our children are different to dogs in terms of their brain's capacity to process and remember, but we humans have more in common with other social mammals than we often like to think. My recent lessons with Hendrix are in line with what has been most helpful with my children. The grown-up approach of managing myself rather than using external motivators is harder work but the big-picture results, in terms of mature children, make it worth the effort.

In parenting, the biggest downside to relying on rewards and punishments is that our children learn to behave according to who's watching. This can leave them immaturely struggling to put in effort simply because it seems the right thing to do. The child or teen comes to look at their conduct in terms of what's in it for them or how they can avoid something unpleasant. Can you see how this doesn't take a child very far in developing an inner, thinking guidance system?

A parent who puts effort into clarifying their own values and doesn't waver from these in how they behave with their child, is likely to be more effective than one who relies on techniques directed at their children. This focus on the self of the parent rather than the child is conveyed through the language and action around the 'I': 'Here's where *I* stand on this issue and this is what *I* will do to back this up' rather than 'Here's what *you* should do and this is what will happen to you if *you* don't obey'.

Getting clearer about an 'I' position

The following are the key principles for holding an 'I' position. The parent:

» manages themself, not the child;

» doesn't try to control what's beyond their own choice to activate;

» doesn't expect words to achieve much and is willing to action what they say;

» doesn't crowd a child's developmental breathing space by pushing or pulling them into behaving as they desire.

The following are some examples of what might typically be said to a child by a parent, and how each might be replaced with a response that better reflects an 'I' position:

'You must stop doing that or I will send you to your room' might be replaced with: 'I am going to have to go to another room because I can't concentrate on this task while there's so much noise.'

'If you stop that screaming now I will buy you a treat at the checkout' can be replaced with: 'I'm not going to keep shopping with all that fuss. If the screaming keeps up I will go straight home. I'll come back and do the shopping later instead of going to the park this afternoon.'

'I will give you extra pocket money if you do an hour of homework each night' is replaced with: 'I see it as your responsibility to satisfy the school's requirements, and I will not step in at the last minute if you haven't managed to get things done on time.'

'If you don't stop fighting with your brother I'm going to take away your PlayStation' is switched to: 'I expect that you two need to learn how to play together cooperatively and I believe you can find a way to do it. If I come back in 5 minutes and you still haven't worked it out, I won't be willing to keep the computers on for the rest of the day.'

'How dare you swear at me? You're grounded!' can be replaced with: 'I'm not willing to be generous when I experience so much disrespect. I am pulling out from giving you that lift to your friend's house today.'

'Okay, I can see from your blank look that you aren't getting far with that homework and it's due tomorrow; let me help you out' is switched to: 'I'm hearing your complaints about this assignment. I'm willing to let you talk it through with me when I've finished my task, but I'm not willing to do any of the work for you.'

'Will you stop that whinging right now or I'll stop all our visits to the park this week!' is replaced with no reaction from the parent, who continues to go about their own business.

'Great job! That's the best drawing of a tree I've ever seen. You could be a great artist one day!' is switched to: 'I'm really interested in what you've created; I'd love to hear about your drawing.'

'You deserve a bravery award for changing your group of friends! I know you're going to be so much happier' is expressed more appropriately as: 'I think it's interesting to

get to know new people. What do you think it will be like
getting to know more of the others in your class?'

There is no magic in using the words of the 'I' position. The impact is
not so much in the language but in the parent's inner conviction and
their perseverance to continue to demonstrate this in action. When
responding to a child's achievements, the parent expresses their
genuine interest without trying to make the child feel a certain way.
When the parent takes a stand about inappropriate behaviour, the
child senses the difference of the parent's inner conviction and, after
a time of testing, begins to manage themself better.

It takes some dedicated time to think things through for yourself, to
know what your limits are and how you will live by them. Be prepared
for your child to test out whether you really mean what you are saying
you're willing and not willing to do. And be prepared to do, or not do,
what you have stated. After a period of challenging your resolve, they
will come to appreciate that they are dealing with an adult who is not
having a knee-jerk reaction but is clear and trustworthy.

Adolescents confronting us with our immaturity

Keeping a focus on our thinking and behaviour as parents is
especially difficult when parenting teenagers. Sometimes adolescent
behaviours are full of so much impulsivity and intense emotion that
we turn all our attention to trying to manage them. Many parents tell
me that they wish they could fast forward the years that their children
are thirteen through to eighteen. While it's easy to be derailed during
our children's adolescence, this phase also provides some valuable
practice opportunities for bringing our maturity up a notch.

Christine's effort to be more of a resource to her seventeen-year-
old son Tom provides a good example. When I met with Christine,

she was beside herself with worry about Tom. He had been staying up most nights sitting in front of his computer and was becoming increasingly moody and verbally aggressive with family members, especially his mum. Tom had grudgingly agreed to see his school counsellor in response to his mum's pressure, but Christine wanted to look at what she too could do to help her son. I asked her what had taken up most of her energies with Tom lately. Christine answered: 'My biggest worry has been Tom's school work. It was such a shock last year to see his report with his grades dropping so much. I've always believed that, of all my children, Tom was the bright one with great potential.'

I then asked Christine how she had responded to Tom's change in his results.

> I've been trying to motivate him and to get his study habits to an acceptable level. We have spent a lot of time together developing a study schedule that will help him to get back on track. I check in on him every now and then to see if he needs my help. I just know that his self-esteem will drop if his grades don't get back to what he is used to.

Christine and I explored together what aspects of her parenting were working and what strategies were not showing signs of helpfulness. She could see that not many of her helping efforts were actually assisting Tom or her relationship with him. With this awareness she set about getting back her clarity about her own responsibilities as Tom's mother. The following is a brief summary of the changes she made within herself in order to be a better resource to her son. Christine expressed to Tom:

I can see that it is not possible for me to make you do your work. How much work you put in is a decision that I see as entirely in your hands. I will be available to help you if you need it but I won't crowd your space. I certainly will not continue to allow the computer and Internet access to be on after I go to bed. I realise that if I don't step in and switch off our connection, I am a part of the problem of allowing computer time to come ahead of reasonable rest.

Christine stopped her practice of always supplying extra money for socialising and unlimited use of her car under all circumstances. She expressed that if she did not feel respected in terms of verbal attacks, she would not supply whatever he asked for. On the occasions when it was not convenient for her to let Tom use the car she would drive him to his friend's place and stop for a coffee together on the way.

It was extremely anxiety-provoking for Christine to step back from trying to direct Tom's study habits, as she was fearful that he would do no work and drop out of school as her younger brother had done. She stayed on track by reminding herself that the old approach was ineffective and seemed to be contributing to Tom's increasing agitation. She knew there were no guarantees that Tom would find his capacity to direct his work efforts but that if he was going to learn this for the future she had to stop intruding and trying to do it for him.

After a few months Christine reported some progress. Tom was less irritated and angry and had thanked his mother for getting off his back about school. His grades did not show much improvement, which was a challenge for Christine. She put a lot of work into calming her fears about Tom's future. To prevent her from cutting off around the school issues, Christine shared with Tom her experience of her brother dropping out of school and how she had realised this had added to her being a bit over the top about Tom's education. She tried to listen with respect and curiosity to his ideas about life after high school without pushing her advice onto him. She was surprised that occasionally Tom would actually ask for her opinion on courses he was interested in.

Christine also turned her attention to her marriage and realised how much she had accommodated her husband, with him becoming increasingly devoted to work while she devoted herself to their children. She started to share with him how hard she was finding the challenges of parenting teenagers. Previously she had focused on telling him what he should say to Tom to address her worries. Christine also allowed her husband much more uninterrupted time with Tom. Previously she had been quick to jump into their relationship to smooth things over whenever she felt that her husband was not handling things sensitively enough.

Pulling it together

Children will have a smoother growing-up trajectory when they have a parent who focuses on being a principled individual. It isn't the goal that both parents become clones of each other, always trying to appear to be on the same page with their child. The reality is that both parents are different individuals and will have varied styles of operating as parents. This helps prepare children for life where adapting to different styles of teachers, and later employees, contributes to their healthy adjustment as adults. So this means that a parent can take the focus off trying to correct or co-opt support from their parenting partner, as well as trying to direct the child, and simply make a project out of maturing themself.

The following checklist is a summary of what's involved when parents attend to themselves and give their children breathing space to manage their own growing-up challenges. Remember that it's an ideal we are unlikely to fully reach, but it can help us to know that our efforts are heading in the direction of maturity. And these efforts contribute to a more mature cycle of reactions in the parent–child relationship.

» Decision-making about what the child needs is not driven by the feelings of the moment but by thoughtfully acquired principles.
» Both parents willingly share their thinking about parenting and listen carefully to the other. Neither assumes that they know best. Each lives by the principle that they are responsible for thinking things through for themselves.
» Each parent can talk to the other about his or her anxieties about being adequate parents but they do not expect the other to relieve these for them. Each is a listening resource to the other without feeling compelled to take responsibility for the other.
» Each parent can relate to the child from a place of self-awareness and without unfounded fears about the child's wellbeing. Hence they are positive about the child without anxiously perceiving the child as needing special attention and praise.
» Both parents enjoy discussing their child and experience pleasure in watching the child develop. However, neither is preoccupied with the child and each can find time for themselves and their marriage.
» Parents are clear about the limits of what they will do for their child.
» Each parent is comfortable allowing the other to manage his or her relationship with the child. They are not drawn into

intervening to take over from the other parent or criticising the parenting of the other.

» Each parent takes responsibility for their own efforts to be a principled parent and doesn't look to the other parent to fill in their confidence gaps.

» Each parent attends to the tensions in their marriage by expressing their ideas without blame. They know that working on any stuck points in their marriage is the most useful thing they can do to not confuse their parenting.

The mature parent, who is reliably present for their child and speaks with conviction about what they will or will not do, doesn't give their child scope for lots of emotional reaction. It's fascinating to see how predictably a child will listen to a parent speaking a thoughtful 'I will not' message, as predictably as the child will not listen to an anxious 'you will not' message.

Have you noticed this difference in the attentiveness of children and adolescents to a parent or teacher? Do you recognise that glazed-over look in the face of a thirteen-year-old as their parent lectures them about what they must do? Very often you can see a child respond to pushing and pulling with a counter-reaction or a half-hearted compliance. What a contrast to observe a child tune into an adult who is being clear about what they will not do. This child, who sees their parent's certainty in the position they take, is left to consider their own responsibility. Herein lies the key to how grown-up parents facilitate grown-up children.

Questions for reflection

» Do I put more energy into managing myself as a responsible parent or trying to shape my children?
» Do I know what I am and am not willing to do when one of my children behaves irresponsibly? How much of my parenting is couched in 'you' messages compared with 'I' messages?
» What issues have I avoided addressing with my spouse and have replaced with attention onto one or more of my children? Is my conversation with my spouse more about us or more about our children?

part 3

Being a
GROWN-UP
beyond our
FAMILY

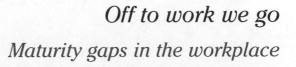

9.

Off to work we go

Maturity gaps in the workplace

'I realised the degree to which I had infantilized the staff members by instructing them and even functioning for them, while I had been irresponsible in failing to do other things that came within my own area.'[1]

—Murray Bowen MD

'The emotional system is the way all the people in the organization relate to each other, respond to each other, react to each other, encourage each other, and get on each other's nerves. It is the silent buzz you feel in the air when you get off the elevator and it creates what we call the "hidden challenge" of leadership because people are so rarely aware of it.'[2]

—Leslie Ann Fox MA and Katharine Gratwick-Baker PhD

I can be really mature at work. Let me set the context in which I function at my best. It's when things are pretty calm, when I'm feeling in control of things and when my business is financially stable. If I add to these ingredients a good dose of people validating the work I'm doing, I can be sure that I'm conducting myself in a truly adult manner. There's a problem with this as I'm sure you can see. These conditions that make it easy for me to function well are rarely present for long. At any moment there can be a shot of tension in a disagreement with a staff member, a few balls dropped as I realise I have tried to juggle too much, a downturn in referrals or some critical feedback. My seemingly calm, clear inner adult can go out the window pretty quickly.

With tension in the air, I get into some familiar immature patterns, doing things just like I did in my family growing up when the heat was on. I start getting busier, taking on more tasks as my way of reducing anxiety through a pretend sense of control. In the process I begin to take over jobs that belong to others. I might look like I am being 'wonder woman' in juggling many projects but beneath the surface my anxiety-driven behaviour doesn't paint a pretty picture. While over-functioning in the big projects I end up neglecting some important duties, such as keeping my paperwork up to date. As the overworking cycle ramps up, I add a dose of micro-management where I stick my nose into other people's tasks, making suggestions about how they should do their job. Before long, I am feeling overloaded and my immaturity really comes to the fore. I start feeling irritable and increase my time spent on critical thoughts about some colleagues. This is followed by my withdrawal from them in an effort to get some emotional breathing space. By this stage, I'm vulnerable to focusing on others' faults and not considering just how much I've contributed to the stress patterns.

I know that I certainly wouldn't want to work with me under these conditions. It's fine for me to be clear about my understanding of each person's job duties, but it isn't fine for me to jump in and take over whenever I feel anxious about the workplace. At these times there's plenty for me to address within my own job description, without me taking over the duties of others.

Over- and under-responsibility

When tension mounts at work or in any relationship system, there are those who react to the tension with lowered energy levels and those, like myself, who react with increased energy. It's easy to think that the increased energy is a positive thing, but because it's driven by anxiety it gets directed in unhelpful ways which get in the way of others working well.

Let me give you a little example of my tendency to take over for others as a way of filling my own maturity gaps. Some time ago I asked an employee at my practice what ideas she had to promote her services to referrers now that she had extended her hours. She suggested that she would organise visits to some doctors to introduce herself. I agreed to send a mail-out on behalf of our institute to update our referral network on our expanded team of counsellors. After the meeting I found myself wondering if my colleague had followed through or whether she was procrastinating. I began to direct unnecessary energy to mentally questioning her ability to follow through and to whether I had left too much on her shoulders. I wondered whether I should be sharing the work of visiting doctors. After one week I asked how it had been going and heard that there had not been time to carry through with phone calls and visits. I immediately jumped in to suggest that I would make a few phone calls. To my colleague's credit, she came back to me the following day and said she had a strategy worked out to do the networking and that she didn't need my help. At that moment, I realised that directing energy towards perceiving my colleague's weaknesses led me to behave more like a patronising parent rather than a respectful professional peer.

To regain any semblance of maturity I need to recognise that I've taken my package of my original family patterns with me into my workplace. When stress increased in my family I relieved some of my tension by trying to help out everyone else. The pattern starts as being overly helpful and accommodating to others to reduce my discomfort. This can easily transition to becoming critical of those whose work I have begun to take over. Recognising this immature pattern, and the problem it causes for others, is the first step to being able to redirect my behaviours when stress gets ramped up at work. My efforts go into being responsible for *my* duties (not those of others) and staying clear with others about what I am committed to in my efforts. When others are struggling to manage, for whatever reason, I work to be in contact with them and really listen to their viewpoints about what they can and can't manage. I need to watch my tendency to encourage a stressed colleague to take a break from some of their contracted duties; this is my learnt pattern of making allowances for others and taking over in order to resume a state of harmony with them.

Steps to maturity for the over-controller at work

Here are some tips for those of us who tend to take over or over-accommodate at work:

» Recognise when you are thinking and doing the job for others and not for yourself.
» Look at what you are neglecting about your responsibilities.
» Tolerate the discomfort of things not going smoothly for others so that they get a chance to deal with their own problems.
» Refrain from trying to manage work that is beyond your direct influence.

If you were prone to problem-solving for others in your family at anxious times, it can be difficult to prevent yourself from falling into the same pattern with work colleagues. Similarly, if you were used to others problem-solving for you in the family, it can be difficult to take responsibility for your own self-direction at work.

Can you see what's wrong with being a problem-solver for others at work? Many people assume that this is exactly what a good leader does: helping others through challenges and assisting them in lifting their performance. I've come to appreciate that there are two key traps to taking on the responsibilities of others. The first is that the other person is less likely to develop their own capacity to manage the dilemmas of their work role. Secondly, the overly helpful colleague is prone to neglecting important aspects of their own responsibilities. Often the over-controller is prone to burnout as their life energy is so focused on others that they lose their self-awareness. The over-controller can see problems in others but may fail to recognise the warning signs of their own fatigue and loneliness in their lack of teamwork. They may be admired by others, which can feel like compensation for the exhaustion, but there is a cost to their own health and to others who are robbed of respectful breathing space to solve their own problems.

Under-functioning in the workplace

Those who react to tension at work with a drain in energy and lowered ability to follow through on tasks are usually in a circular dance with an over-functioner. One gives up their capacity to manage to the one who steadies themself by appearing capable. Both sides of the relationship inadvertently reinforce each other in their instinctive tension-relieving position in relationships. One pulls back from tasks while the other takes on more. One feels some relief through distancing themself while the other feels relief through being helpful.

The person at work who is prone to dropping their functioning at stressful times is vulnerable to being criticised and scapegoated by others, and to feel increasingly like an outsider from their team. This is a really hard pattern to reverse as withdrawing feels like such an attractive way of coping with relational pressure.

Richard's challenge

One example of someone who found themselves in this difficult withdrawal cycle at work was 37-year-old Richard, who worked as a physiotherapist at a rehabilitation centre. He regularly found himself collapsed at work whenever he sensed performance pressure. I recall him reflecting on how different he was at work to the way he functioned at home and in his community activities:

> It's so frustrating for me that I can be so relaxed and confident with my friends, my wife and at the football club, but at work I sit in meetings and can't even think of one useful thought. I go blank and I'm terrified that I'll be asked to say what I think and I'll have nothing useful to say. It's like I'm two different people at work and at home.

The challenge for Richard was that his difficulty managing at work created so much distress that it started to seep into his confidence in other parts of his life. In tackling this challenge he first came to understand why this pattern was so hard to change. He'd tried lots of psychology techniques to correct his thoughts and get some distance from his anxiety but it only made a minor dent in his emotional emptiness at work.

For Richard and many others, this blueprint of withdrawal has been wired into them through their childhood family relationship patterns. They've become unconsciously accustomed to distancing themselves in the face of challenge and subtly inviting others to fill their space and carry their load. Richard was highly sensitive to not meeting his father's expectations and would walk on eggshells around his dad to avoid any upset. His mother had focused on bolstering Richard's insecurity by praising him regularly, but she had also invited him to assist her in keeping his dad calm. The biggest outbursts Richard can remember from his growing up were around him not doing well enough at school. His mother would suggest that he needed to improve his school grades to keep Dad happy.

The story of Richard's parents and their families of origin shed light on what had contributed to so much intense anxiety about upsetting family harmony, and how much of this anxiety was wrapped up in educational success. As Richard appreciated what was behind his withdrawals and overwhelming feelings of inadequacy at work, he could tolerate making slow progress towards being more his own person. He could see how his sensitivity to meeting work expectations was getting in the way of him being a separate self. He also realised how much his search for praise and help from rescuing colleagues was not going to help him make any progress. He expressed what he's learnt by saying:

> I've got to stop beating myself up about my failures at work and just accept that this is always going to be a stressful area for me. It's going to take time to reduce the way I shut down and how reliant I've become on others filling in the gaps for me. I know I'm not stupid, but I also know that I get lost in relationships at work and just let others take over. I wish it was easier but I can do better at staying involved in team meetings even when my emotions are pushing me to shut down.

Richard really turned a corner in his self-awareness in seeing that the problem was not in him as an individual. It was in the space between all individuals at work who react to stress in different ways.

For those who withdraw and get easily overwhelmed at times of heightened stress, it's easy to become increasingly negative about the organisation and avoidant of those with whom you sense disapproval. The maturity challenge here is to focus on tasks and not on the uncomfortable feelings. The under-functioner at work needs to see how they unconsciously contribute to inviting others to take over for them and how their tendency to distance themselves adds to others' reactivity towards them.

Steps to maturity for the under-functioner at work

Here are some tips to help with lifting functioning rather than allowing others to take over:

» Recognise when others are thinking for you and doing parts of your job responsibilities.

» Push past the feelings of negativity in the face of others' expectations of you and get clear about your priority tasks.

» When others seem intimidating in the way they articulate about work, take care not to shut down your own effort to think things through and contribute your ideas.

» When others start taking over your work, practise making it clear that you are willing to do this yourself.

» Tolerate the discomfort of staying connected to colleagues when things feel pressured. Initiate casual chats at break times. Be as present as possible at meetings and team events.

How to have a mature balance of family and work

The lopsided patterns of functioning at work are similar to what happens between many spouses at home. One spouse takes over most of the relationship work in the family, leaving the other to be more of an avoider or outsider. Another spouse deals with insecurities by distancing themself and becoming more dominant in public arenas. This is a circular pattern that is not caused by one person. Often the outsider at home can be an insider at work and put a disproportionate amount of focus on job success to the detriment of family. Conversely, the insider at home often struggles to find the energy and direction they'd like to have in their creative pursuits, community involvement or career.

This pattern of uneven balance in functioning makes it very hard for two adults to achieve satisfaction in their family relationships and in their work. Both husbands and wives can feel disillusioned about this and become critical of their spouse for putting too much energy into either work or home life. They each fail to see how they have played their part in putting too much focus on one part of their life and have accommodated the other, filling the gaps for them. Remember that solid maturity is promoted when a person addresses their roles in a variety of domains; it's not just about being a high achiever in one area at the expense of our partners who are filling our gaps in the other important parts of adult life.

A person who puts effort into being responsible in their family is likely to be more mature in their balance at work. They are less likely to overwork and prop up others. They don't get in the way of others carving out their own space in which to work efficiently and creatively. They think as much about their role as a spouse and a parent as they do about their work role; and their contribution is equally valued both at work and at home.

Triangles at work: a detour from having to grow up

Workplaces, like families, have regular periods of anxiety. This tension is inevitable when you throw together very different people to spend large quantities of time bumping up against each other. One of the easiest ways for us to manage work tensions is to find someone with whom we can vent about another. Can you recognise this as the beginning of forming a relationship triangle? When dealing with differences with a workmate it's easy to lower stress by finding colleagues who agree with our negative view of that person. Gossiping about the people we find difficult, and finding others to side with our view, is the fastest way to feel calm about the problem. However, this pathway to stress relief doesn't require us to find any maturity from within ourselves. Is it any wonder that it's so common to find multiple side-taking groups in workplaces?

Simon's workplace challenges

Simon was an ambitious man in his mid-thirties who had been climbing his way up the ladder of technology companies for the past decade. When I met him, he was confronting a crisis in confidence and wanted to find a way to regain his effectiveness at work. Here's the story he pieced together as he worked to understand the reduction in his coping abilities at work.

Simon had been promoted to team leader of the sales department in a medium-size IT company. He described how he had been excited by the opportunity to learn some management skills. His confidence was boosted by the support he was shown by his fellow team members to take on the role.

Coinciding with Simon's promotion was a downturn in the demand for the company's products and a subsequent team budget cut from head office for the coming year. Everyone's anxiety increased as they felt pressure to work harder with reduced resources. A good deal of team energy went into complaining to each other about the change in the company culture and what they perceived as the focus on profit at the expense of people. Simon had the challenging role of conveying hard senior management decisions to his team. He felt isolated from the wider group and responded by communicating via group emails rather than face to face. His messages about reducing expenses were not popular and he tried hard to minimise face-to-face contact which could put him in the midst of a confrontation. Negativity towards Simon increased within his team and, in response, he began to distance himself by working away from the office. He'd always seen himself as a warm and sociable person but he was now hearing complaints, via the human resources manager, that he was being perceived as highly strung and difficult.

Simon fantasised about resigning and shifting companies but he did sense that there were lessons to be learnt if he could hang in there and figure out what he could do to get out of his negative cycle. In getting real about the part he was playing, Simon reflected:

> I can so easily describe the troublemakers who I think are undermining my leadership. They're the ones I've become ultra sensitive to and I'm avoiding them in all sorts of ways. But if I keep my energy going towards blaming these individuals, I'm just going to add to my uptightness around the office. The more I'm avoiding the problem people, the more I am playing favourites with the people who I'm not threatened by. If I don't find a way to change my reactions, I'm going to keep digging a bigger hole for myself.

Simon had started to gain awareness about the part he was playing in the divisions and scapegoating in his department. He noted that his way of dealing with tension in the family he grew up in was very similar to his 'keep out of the way' method of dealing with tensions at work. This helped him to see that his distancing was part of his programmed reactivity. If he could modify this behaviour he might be able to stop adding fuel to the team tension. Simon's efforts went into reducing his favouritism and his avoidance of the less affirming team members. These were critical steps for him to get out of triangles that were keeping him from resolving his leadership problems.

De-triangling strategies for work

Here are some ways that Simon used his awareness of triangles to extricate himself from them.

Favour one-to-one contact with key individuals

Simon began to work on changing his part in the negative downturn in team morale. He stopped communicating important policy changes through group emails and began to meet individually with team members. He went into each conversation with an effort to be clear about his principles. This assisted him to state the facts in an open manner and give each person the opportunity to talk through the implications for them. He was clear about what he could not change about company policy but was open to suggestions from the team about how to best deal with the changes.

Be careful about venting your view of others

Simon stopped meeting with his HR manager to seek support and validation from a third party about those he perceived as his 'enemies'. Instead, he made every effort to take any dilemma in his work relationships directly to the person it belonged with. Simon felt the inner pull to avoid spending time with those he knew had been complaining about his leadership, but he determined that this would be a repeat of his family distancing pattern. Distancing was only going to increase the tensions in relationships.

Move closer and keep genuinely connected

Simon found the courage to reverse his avoidance of those who were not supporting him. He made regular attempts to chat casually with each of these people about non-anxious topics, such as what they did on their weekends. He found out more about those he had distanced from and began to chat with them about their hobbies and their families. The effort to stay in friendly contact, in the midst of a tense time, was one of the most growth-producing experiences that Simon could remember. The more he kept contact with individuals on the team, the more he noticed his agitation levels decrease. While the financial and workload pressures were still as real, Simon found that he was less tense about his new role and began to be able to switch off from work at home and sleep better.

* * *

Work had provided Simon with a valuable laboratory for testing efforts to increase his maturity. Taking the above three steps to remove himself from triangles, and being more of a separate individual who was in contact with others, showed him that there are better options than running away from difficult workplace dynamics.

Maintaining balance between connection and conviction

It's easy to confuse keeping contact with work colleagues as a form of creating a false sense of harmony or even fusion. Some workplaces put so much energy into creating a type of happy family that there's little energy left for individuals to get on with their job duties. Those who have cut off from their extended families are especially prone to creating a substitute family at work.

The key to distinguishing whether interactions at work are part of healthy connection or unhealthy fusion is to ask whether differences are being aired directly. When there is too much 'togetherness' fusion there is little tolerance for disagreement. In contrast, when there is mature relating, people are free to both engage in warm banter and to express their different viewpoints respectfully. In Simon's efforts to mature himself as a leader, he not only worked at reversing his distancing pattern but also at being able to speak his opinion on a work assignment, even when he knew it would not be popular. In this way, he put as much effort into connecting with others as he put into holding his own convictions, which were grounded in thoughtful workplace principles. He worked at lowering his tendency to be dogmatic in holding to his opinions. This opened up his capacity to be ready to revise his views if others shared new and useful information that he hadn't previously considered.

Mature leadership can come from any level

The following is a summary of mature leadership characteristics as described in Bowen's family systems theory.[3] These are the qualities that Simon worked hard at actioning to reverse his downward spiral of ineffective leadership. You don't need to be in an official leadership position in an organisation in order to bring these qualities to work. Any person in a group who exercises these attributes will add to lifting the maturity of the group as a whole. Imagine what a valuable contribution you can bring to your workplace when you:

» have the courage to speak and act according to your own clear principles;

» care about benefiting others as much as yourself;

» are not emotionally dominating;

» put energy into improving yourself in the service of improving the organisation;

» are clear about your work without telling others how to do their work;

» are open to changing direction after considering others' opinions thoughtfully;

» know how to move out of the way so that others' strengths can come through;

» are not swept along by the force of impulsive ideas of others.

Giving up the quest for the quick fix

In the workplace, as in all relationship systems, we will do well to accept that there are no quick fixes to anxiety escalations. This isn't easy to acknowledge when the marketplace is flooded with fads for miraculously improving your performance and leadership excellence at work. The fact that there are so many new packages for workplace transformation is evidence that these quick fixes don't stand the test of time. The challenge of growing up is learning to tolerate the slow pace of change — in contrast to the child who wants instant responses. It means you will sometimes find it lonely to stay on your value-directed course when the pressure to revert to creating false togetherness is intense.

This process of being mature in an anxious organisation has been likened to learning to sail against the wind; and as any sailor will tell you, this requires concentration and tolerating some tension as the wind pressures the vessel to let it take over the controls. Good skippers know how to tolerate sufficient tension to keep a steady course. They don't try to overpower their vessel with too much sail in order to get to the finish line faster, as they know this will inevitably knock them backwards. They also know not to panic and retreat to the safe harbour of familiarity. They focus on their key tasks of setting the course and letting the crew know their intensions so that each person can get on with focusing on their own tasks. There's only one path to growing this ability: through patient, thoughtful perseverance in the midst of experience … no short cuts to be found.

Questions for reflection

» What are my patterns when the stress and tension levels go up at work? Am I prone to doing too much or doing too little? How does this affect me and others at work?

» Do I have a balance between my family and my work responsibilities? In what parts of my life am I over-working and where am I under-working?

» What people do I vent to at work to lower my anxiety about others? How can I reduce my triangling and have more contact with the individuals I find difficult?

» How much of my workplace energy goes into creating a substitute family?

» Am I comfortable with disagreements with those I work with? What's my balance between staying in contact with others and keeping my work principles clear?

10.

Developing mature beliefs

Compliance, rebellion or examination

'The pseudo self is made up of ... beliefs and principles acquired through the relationship system in the prevailing emotion ... beliefs [are] borrowed from others or accepted in order to enhance one's position in relationship to others.'[1]

—Murray Bowen MD

'We will no longer be infants, tossed back and forth by the waves, and blown here and there by every wind of teaching ...'[2]

—The apostle Paul

How have you developed your inner thinking guidance system? Where do you go to get clear principles that give you a touch point for making decisions during stressful times and to keep you reasonably steady when facing setbacks? Have you borrowed your beliefs from others as part of being connected to a group? Or have you worked out what ideas you think are worthy of your allegiance through a process of independent examination?

Each chapter of this book on adult maturity has mentioned the value of considering carefully what values and ethics you choose to guide your behaviour and help you act consistently. When it comes to beliefs, it's simple to go along with the viewpoint of your majority group, your parents, your cultural group or your peer group. If you're carrying unaddressed resentments towards your parents there may be a tendency to take on beliefs that are the opposite of theirs. Whether you adopt beliefs to comply with or to rebel against others, in each scenario there isn't much thought and effort going into the process. This leads to beliefs that are superficial. They can chop and change according to the emotions of the group you're in. Such pseudo beliefs won't hold much benefit for you in determining how to make a difficult choice when you are under pressure. They won't help you to take a position on what you believe are important issues if you are easily thrown off course by another's disapproval.

When was the last time you felt strongly about a political or social issue? I wonder if you have recently taken a maturity test on how you have come to these strong views. Prompted by the challenge of practising what I'm writing about, I recently took a new policy proposal being debated in the media and decided to do some independent thinking to investigate my own position. I began with a certainty that the proposal was a good one; it sounded reasonable on the surface and had the support of the political party I usually vote for. There were plenty of opinion pieces which captured my eye that supported my view. I found myself skipping over any headline that discussed it from another angle. In pulling myself up from taking such a lazy path to my opinion, I decided to take the time to read the original policy statements and not the opinions of others about it. To my surprise I read details of the proposal and the rationale behind it that were not being discussed in the popular press. By the time I had looked at the fine print of the policy my view had shifted completely. This was not what I'd expected. It was a maturity wake-up call as I realised how easily I develop my view from my subjective biases and not from my intellect.

Do we just follow our family's traditions?

Every family has a depth of religious and cultural traditions that spans many generations. Such traditions can reveal lots of rich information about our family's unique story of survival and cohesion over centuries. Who wouldn't want to tap into such a valuable window onto our past? On the other hand, it is worth asking whether it helps us grow up if we just go along with these traditions without any examination.

At the age of 38, Henry was considering marrying his long-term girlfriend Carla. This was challenging him to consider what kind of marriage he wanted to have. Would he get married in the Catholic church of his parents or have a civil ceremony? Henry had nonchalantly assumed his parents' identification with the Catholic church but hadn't investigated for himself what his own beliefs were. When I asked Henry what thought he had put into deciding which tradition represented his beliefs he exclaimed: 'Gosh, I just haven't thought about the Catholic church's teachings since my school days. I got so much of it drummed into me then that it's been a relief not to think about it as an adult.'

Henry went on to reflect on a good friend of his who was very involved in a church community and could explain his beliefs intelligently. He envied his friend's clarity of faith and resolved to investigate his options for belief along with the religion of his family tradition. Henry determined that before he began planning his wedding with Carla, it was timely to explore his parents' stories about adopting their beliefs. He realised that it would be more adult to choose rather than unconsciously inherit his beliefs.

Henry's mother was a staunch Catholic who had been the driving force behind her children's baptisms, confirmations and Catholic school attendance. In talking to his parents, Henry noted that his father converted to Catholicism at the age of 60. Interested to discover his father's reasons behind the timing of his conversion, Henry discovered that his dad had waited until after the death of his mother-in-law, Henry's grandmother. She had vehemently opposed her daughter marrying a non-Catholic. Henry's father felt compelled not to base his decision to convert on just appeasing his mother-in-law. It was useful for Henry to consider how beliefs and relationships can get so tangled up. He could see how the timing and basis of his father's decisions about religion were partly tied up with relationship tensions that had never been resolved.

Henry spent a good deal of time checking to see whether his decision about where to get married would be driven by relationship issues or from his own examination of faith. An awareness of his desire for his mother's approval assisted Henry in using both his emotions and intellect in considering his beliefs.

Two problems with fast-tracked beliefs

There are two maturity pitfalls that come from borrowing beliefs from the groups we want to be part of: dogmatism and avoidance. Spiritual and philosophical beliefs that are adopted as an instant package can promote an exaggerated certainty that gets stirred up by the emotions of wanting to belong in relationships. This can result in expressions of dogmatic fundamentalism and a refusal to engage with those who have different views. People with dissimilar beliefs are viewed as a threat to their group cohesion. Reactions to outsiders are likely to be hostile and inflated.

The second maturity block is an inability to express a considered and logical view on many important ethical issues. When we get lazy and stop investigating the facts behind our opinions, we're prone to taking on the views of whoever we like reading or listening to at the time. This might be a persuasive voice on talkback radio or an articulate friend whom we aspire to be like. When we get caught in this 'go with the flow' attitude we're left with very little depth to our viewpoints. In order to cover up this vulnerability, we're likely to avoid conversations about religion, philosophy, social issues and politics. The common rationale for this evasion is that these issues are personal and should not be allowed to upset a social gathering. The other justification for avoiding exposing our lack of clarity is the pluralist idea that all belief systems are pretty much the same and that the world would be a better place without any thoughtful critical comparisons.

You don't have to look very far to see examples of both of these maturity problems. It might be on this evening's news where a representative of a religious group is condemning anyone who speaks against an aspect of their religion. Perhaps you will see it closer to home when a family member quickly changes the subject when a political topic is raised in dinner table conversation. Theologian and philosopher Douglas Wilson has described these maturity problems well in saying that, 'Those who blindly follow traditions and those who blindly throw traditions overboard share at least ignorance in common. One keeps what he does not know, another throws away what he does not know.'[3]

The key maturity challenge is to get beyond blind acceptance or rejection of any set of beliefs and values. This asks a great deal of us. In particular, it asks us to take time to reflect on what we believe and what creed we live by. It's not easy to carve out reflection time in this pressured world. It sure is easier to come to conclusions based on subjective whims and what brings us the most comfort and acceptance from others.

Is there room for emotions and intellect?

The area of spirituality is not easy to be objective about. It often comes down to one person's subjective experience alongside another's. Are emotional experiences a sufficient basis for mature beliefs? What about examining contradictions in religious and philosophical writings? What about thinking through the historical basis of a belief system? The growing-up challenge is not to just consider the content of any belief system but, more importantly, to think about the process of coming to a set of beliefs. Have we adopted or rejected a religion based on a reaction to others or based on a thoughtful exploration on our own behalf? This is the key question whether we are considering our ethics, our politics, our views about the origins of the universe or what gives life purpose.

My own spiritual faith grew out of a subjective experience of what I perceived to be the presence of God in my life during my growing-up years. This personal relationship experience has been important in my growth of faith; but this emotional experience alone hasn't been sufficient for me to have an adult confidence in the basis of my beliefs. The most useful growing-up opportunity has been when I confronted doubts about my childhood adoption of Christianity. In my thirties I was curious to understand the basis of other people's beliefs that appeared cohesive for them. This compelled me to explore the teachings that formed the foundation of other faiths. It was a maturing exercise to take a childhood faith and put it under the scrutiny of critical comparison. Reading and comparing the basis of other religions has taken my belief system beyond my personal experience. I have gained an appreciation for aspects of beauty that can be found in other religions. At the same time I have increased my intellectual respect for the historical grounds and depth of the faith from my childhood. While my clarity of belief has increased, so has my desire to be able to enjoy a healthy connection with those who have different convictions.

To be honest, I don't find it easy to be calm when I'm talking with people who strongly disagree with my views — but it does give me really good growing-up practice to learn to be more comfortable with difference. The emergence of the new atheism in the Western world has provided a really useful set of articulate arguments to grapple with in an adult manner. If I'm afraid to examine these beliefs about a godless universe alongside my own viewpoint about a creator God, it doesn't say much for the maturity of my position. When taking a mature approach to religion, we stay open to reviewing our own beliefs, not in light of flavour-of-the-moment ideas but in comparison to logic and evidence.

It's not unusual to think that overlooking differences and viewing all beliefs as sharing common ground is a mature stance. It's worth asking, however, whether this is a thoughtful position or an anxiously driven desire for pseudo harmony. A desire to blur distinctions may be more about discomfort with being in contact with different views, driven by a togetherness force, rather than a conclusion drawn from examining the basis of different views. Theologian and historian John Dickson makes this point in stating that 'by seeking to affirm the sameness of the world religions [we] … are in danger of honouring none of them. As unpopular as the idea appears to have become, we simply must allow the world religions to have their distinct voice and to express their different points of view.'[4]

Where psychology and faith can diverge

I wouldn't be surprised if you were puzzled right now about why a book that is grounded mostly in a psychological theory is diverging into matters of spirituality. I think that theories of human behaviour and psychological health run the risk of leaving out an important marker of maturity: the capacity to admit your own wrongdoing. There is a potential for psychological explanations to be a block to growing up because they can be used to excuse damaging and irresponsible behaviour.

In the mid 1970s Karl Menninger, a prominent American psychiatrist, raised this problem in asking the question: whatever happened to the concept of sin or wrongdoing? In his book entitled *Whatever Became of Sin?* Dr Menninger questions whether a loss of a public discourse about right and wrong may have contributed to an increasing sense of personal irresponsibility at all levels of society.[5] I think this is a worthy question to ask in thinking about growing up. The immature child is quick to hide and deny their misdeeds and point the finger at another. How many adults continue this same pattern? How often do we cover over selfish acts with excuses?

Personal and social responsibility

If all action that hurts another can be explained away as a type of immaturity or as embedded in intergenerational family patterns, there is a risk of avoiding responsibility for wrong actions and not seeking forgiveness and restitution in a genuine way. It's important to be clear that any psychological understanding of behaviour doesn't reduce personal and social responsibility. Perhaps the ability to recognise our factual failings and say sorry is one of the most vital expressions of growing up. For the people of Australia this was demonstrated in 2008 when then Prime Minister Kevin Rudd delivered a public apology to indigenous Australians for the many injustices done to them under governments in the past. Mr Rudd did acknowledge that an apology means nothing without actions to set things right, but he took a first step by expressing on behalf of many a deep remorse for how our own and past generations had patronised and disenfranchised the original owners of our land. As an Australian, I can see that there is a long way for all of us to go to achieve some real restitution, but making excuses on the basis of past generational ignorance or blaming the oppressed is downright childish.

The growing-up experience of being honest about wrongdoing allows us to forgive those who are sorry about harm done to us. We accept the imperfection in all our fellow humans and are therefore better prepared to let go of bitterness about the effects of others' misconduct towards us. As well as seeing acts of wrongdoing we also can see the system of anxious relationships that contributes to some individuals and groups occupying irresponsible positions. This broader perspective can assist in moving us towards being able to both say sorry and to forgive others. It's easy to write these sentences or speak these words about being sorry, but it is perhaps the hardest maturity challenge to really live out genuine remorse, apology, reparation and honest forgiveness.

Unhealthy guilt or mature contrition

I meet many people in counselling who carry an unhealthy burden of guilt and find themselves saying sorry for everything that upsets another. This isn't the kind of apologising I am talking about here. Mature remorse requires examination of the facts of how we have behaved as opposed to following our feelings of inadequacy. I've found it helpful to hold two levels of awareness: one is to see my patterns of behaviour that come from anxious programming in my original family — patterns that can only be addressed gradually; the second is to see the behaviour that disrespects or harms others and requires an actioned apology. Examples of such behaviours are dishonesty, gossiping, backhanded putdowns or neglecting to be generous to others. For such things I need to have a code of right and wrong rather than a psychological theory that absolves me from setting things right in relationships and in society. Yes, it's useful to see that people's failings are influenced by their experience of relationships; it's also constructive to see that we can be accountable for the choices we make. Increased maturity, or differentiation, helps us to hold both perspectives.

Understanding that we all fall short on the scale of maturity is a helpful way of appreciating our deficits in acting from principle rather than from reactions. None of us human beings is anywhere close to having achieved complete maturity; but when a person is prepared to work on themself and not simply try to fit in with others, they can know that they're on a path to growing up. This is the good news: that if you can see and acknowledge your errors, your sins, and make reparations, you can bring some mature humility to your relationships.

Figuring out our inner thinking guidance system

To let go of our immature child we need a strong set of principles to hold us when our frustrations are trying to take us over. To prevent versions of childish tantrums we need a conscious code of ethics. To deal with the inevitable suffering in life, without giving up, we will benefit from having worked out a sense of purpose and meaning. The tricky part is teasing out what opinions are independent of relationship sensitivities that feed mindless compliance or rebellion. Until you can separate out what are your own beliefs from what is tied up with being part of a family group (or substitute family group), you can't make much progress in maturity. Additionally, unless you've worked on your inner guidance system and have a line to hold, you can't get very far in improving your relationships. The demands in terms of time and effort may seem too weighty and unrealistic. On the other hand, the benefits in terms of steadiness of self in the face of challenge, a sense of direction and health in relationships, make a compelling case for doing the work of developing a mature set of beliefs.

Questions for reflection

» How much do I know about my family's beliefs and traditions? How have family members determined what they believe? Have they come to their beliefs for the sake of harmony or have they independently figured out their faith and ethics?

» How much have I adopted or rejected my family's beliefs and ethics without personal investigation? What could I do to consider my own guidance system in a thoughtful way?

» Are my spiritual beliefs embedded in subjective experience or are they balanced with thinking about evidence and logic?

» Do I get uncomfortable and avoid the issue of my selfishness and wrongdoing? What do I want to be the factual basis for knowing if I have wronged another and need to make amends?

» How can I make time to unravel my thinking around an important issue, tracing it from its primary source to the position I currently hold, rather than borrowing opinions that are most comfortable to me?

» What steps will I take to explore what gives my life integrity and purpose?

part 4

NURTURING
maturity in the
face of SETBACKS

11.

Separation and divorce

Getting beyond blaming

'The one who runs away ... can have an intense relationship in a marriage, which he sees as ideal and permanent at the time, but the physical distance pattern is part of him. When tension mounts in the marriage, he will use the same pattern of running away.'[1]

—Murray Bowen MD

'Once the relationship is re-established after the usual cut-off represented by divorce, working towards separate boundaries, openness, and an equal stance become as important here as in other relationships.'[2]

—Roberta Gilbert MD

It's interesting to note that divorce rates have climbed dramatically over the past decades at the same time as young adults have more frequently distanced themselves from their parents and romantic expectations of marriage have been intensified by popular media. Seeing a marriage partner as the healing substitute for what we perceive as inadequate nurturing from our parents can put unsustainable pressures on a marriage. When the stresses of managing mortgages and children must inevitably be dealt with in a marriage, the expectations of the other spouse mount and disappointments begin to emerge.

For many marriages these cycles of criticism of the other bring out the worst immaturities of each person. It's all too easy to think that it is the other person who has changed and not to see how both spouses' anxious reactions have contributed to destructive patterns of relating. After years of negative patterns in a marriage, many report that there's just too much water under the bridge to be motivated to rebuild. The challenge after separating is to learn lessons from what went wrong rather than simply to move on with angry blaming of the other.

Getting out of the blame cycle

When Cecelia separated from Evan a storm of emotional drama erupted. After another one of their intense arguments, where doors were being slammed and voices raised to levels that roused the neighbours, Cecelia decided that this was the last straw, particularly as she saw the impact the fights were having on their two young children. She had plenty of support from her parents and siblings to leave Evan and she took up her sister's offer to deliver a letter to Evan at his work to tell him not to come home.

Evan went to live with his parents for a time and made it clear that he had no intention of walking away from his home and his children. At the suggestion of her support network, Cecelia had changed the locks on the house and emailed Evan to let him know she was seeking legal advice about protecting herself and the children. Evan responded with defiance and broke his way into their home while Cecelia was out. The scene was certainly set for an ugly separation struggle.

When I met with Cecelia, the pull was strong to side with her against Evan and to join her other allies in shutting Evan out to ensure hers and the children's safety. While safety issues needed to be objectively considered, it was also clear that the more Cecelia cut off communication from Evan, the more excluded and desperate his position was becoming. When any of us find ourselves in the negative outside position in a relationship triangle, where others are allied against us, it will certainly bring out the worst in our reactive responses. I asked Cecelia to describe the way she had separated and how much she had communicated directly to Evan about her intentions. She could see that all her communication had been through others or indirectly through letters and emails. She reflected on how as her distrust of Evan was increasing her contact with him was decreasing, and how she was beginning to go along with the push from others to take out a restraining order against him.

After thinking about the way she had separated from Evan and its effect, Cecelia began planning ways to meet with him and talk through her decision to separate but to do it in a way that didn't inflame things for her or the children. I recall her moment of realisation that her own behaviours and alliances with her family were actually adding fuel to an already upsetting and stressful time for herself and for Evan. 'I can see that the more I talk to others about our arguments, the more I start to think of Evan as a bastard who can't be trusted,' she explained. 'I know he can seem irrational at times, but I've been pretty irrational in the way I've argued with him.'

Cecelia and Evan had tried counselling to break their patterns of conflict, but Cecelia had lost any hope that they could learn to relate well to each other. She was clear she wanted to separate but she also became clear that she wanted to separate with her own integrity intact. She thought about ways she could keep the discussions about separating and staying in touch with the children as a conversation between herself and Evan. This would mean making every effort not to vent her frustrations about Evan to her family and friends. Cecelia reported that as she and Evan met to discuss their separation it wasn't all smooth sailing. In his distress, Evan accused her of ruining the children's lives and letting her family get between them. Cecelia's usual response would have been to counteract with an attack on Evan's character but she was committed to not adding fuel to the way they related. With her sustained effort not to counterattack or to align against him through third parties, Cecelia could see that it was possible to achieve a mature separation where both she and Evan could talk reasonably about sharing the parenting load.

The path to villainising Evan would have been easy for Cecelia and would have kept the negative intensity of their conflict alive for many years. Cecelia was able to use the distance of more space from Evan to be more thoughtful in her responses rather than turning him into a lifelong enemy. She could see that they had both brought their immaturities to their marriage and contributed to a destructive pattern of 'tit for tat' fighting in their efforts to bolster their insecurities. Rather than blame Evan for everything, Cecelia was able to learn about herself in the wake of the end of her marriage. She was motivated to stay mindful of her lessons about herself so that she wouldn't replicate her patterns in any future relationship.

The challenge of achieving an emotional divorce

It is possible to be legally divorced but to continue for many years without achieving an emotional divorce. A person can remain so hurt and angry with their ex-spouse over many years that they have little energy left for rebuilding their life. While physically separate from each other, it is as if they remain as emotionally sensitive to each other as they were at the point when their marriage fell apart. Seeing the other can evoke the same feeling of upset as happened during the rawness of the legal process.

Raymond had remained cut off from his ex-wife Linda for the past five years. He had tolerated only essential communication about their teenage children's visits and medical and education expenses. When I met Raymond he was struggling with depression. His job and his relationship with his children were unsatisfying. He lived with his elderly mother but spent very little time interacting with her. Much of his energy had been directed to holding out on what he saw as Linda's unreasonable demands for financial assistance. He confided in one of his daughters about his view of her mother's manipulation of him and he gained some comfort from sensing that she was on his side. But he knew he was stuck. His anger about the marriage break-up remained as fresh as the day he came home to an empty house. It was as if he put his hostile feelings into his emotional freezer to maintain their freshness. There had been little thawing of his negative intensity over five years. In the pain of his chronic dissatisfaction with life, Raymond could see that he hadn't grown up at all through the experience of his failed marriage. Because of the pain he was in, he was prepared to explore a different way of dealing with his divorce.

Raymond started by making a bit more contact with Linda and being more flexible about her requests to adjust their children's visiting schedule. He was careful to not dismiss his own wishes to spend quality time with the children but he began to recognise when he was saying no just to stay angry with Linda versus saying no because it didn't work for him. Linda expressed suspicion about what Raymond was up to. Raymond reported that she suggested he must be trying to get out of a financial responsibility, but he persisted in not being reactive and in being more cooperative. He made an effort to speak positively about Linda's best qualities in front of their children.

When he had difficulties handling their sixteen-year-old son's push for independence, Raymond tried using Linda as a resource rather than keep his parenting experiences to himself. He came to discover that Linda had some useful perspectives on handling the kids and, while he didn't see eye to eye with her on all matters, he could see that it was possible for them to become a resource to each other, as opposed to a burden, in parenting adolescents. It took a few months and some ups and downs in the process of being less reactive but Raymond did begin to feel less stuck in his life as he opened up contact with Linda. His moods were improving and he discovered that he had the energy to explore changing his job. The other step Raymond took to get better emotional separation from his ex-marriage was to make contact with his previous parents-in-law. When Linda's mother was hospitalised for cancer treatment he used this as an opportunity to send a card and take the children to visit her.

How making more contact helps to get unstuck

One of the interesting paradoxes of becoming more mature is that making more contact with previously significant people helps to create better boundaries in these relationships. With more contact it's possible to reduce the experience of feeling overwhelmed by anxious sensitivities to others. Raymond certainly discovered that he stopped investing negative life energy into his resentments about his divorce when he started to relate more frequently to his ex-wife. He began to see her as a human being again and his children seemed to become more settled in this new context of cooperation between their parents. At the time of his divorce Raymond had found that angry avoidance of his ex-wife was a way of reducing his anxious insecurities, but five years on this distance was becoming a drain on his resources. Along with many other people who work at learning about themselves after a divorce, he reported a surprising sense of relief in being able to have a reasonable relationship with his ex-wife and her family. Children of such parents are fortunate to have an example of flexibility and willingness to grow in maturity.

Questions for reflection

» To what extent can I see how my marriage problems were compounded by both spouses' reactions?
» Am I fuelling post-separation hostility by inviting others to triangle or take my side against my ex-spouse or by avoiding direct respectful communication with them?
» Am I cutting off or distancing myself in order to manage the pain of a divorce? What are some ways I could regain some energy for personal growth through making an effort to be in calm contact with my ex-spouse?

12.

Symptoms and setbacks

The uneven playing field of maturity

'There are varying degrees of fusion between emotional and intellectual systems in the human. The greater the fusion between emotion and intellect, the more the individual is fused into people around him. The greater the fusion, the more man [the human] is vulnerable to physical illness, emotional illness, and the less he [or she] is able to consciously control his own life.'[1]

—Murray Bowen MD

'Often people think very unfair, punitive, and even violent thoughts towards themselves … If they could think about themselves with the same principles they use towards others, the problem would be solved. They would be on the road to a principled way of being a self.'[2]

—Roberta Gilbert MD

Have you noticed that not everyone who experiences significant hardship experiences the ongoing effects of these setbacks in their lives? Some people, after experiencing a time of struggle, seem to be able to bounce back and rebuild satisfying and productive lives. There are others who seem to slip into the grip of anxiety and depression and struggle to pull up after dealing with a disappointment. Some people go through life with few symptoms to challenge them and the ability to take hold of opportunities as they arise; while others seem to struggle to find stable relationships and to muster sufficient confidence to try anything new.

The common view is that certain temperaments and genetic predispositions explain these variables. While biology certainly goes some way to explaining the variations in resilience from person to person, it is also logical to see that not everyone is dealt the same hand of cards in terms of their maturity.

Maturity or differentiation as a continuum

Individual maturity and resilience from a Bowen systems perspective is viewed on a kind of scale, from relatively high to low. Each of us inherits a degree of maturity, or differentiation of self, from what was available in the family we grew up in. The two key variables to how much maturity we start adulthood with are the amount of relationship maturity in our family of origin and how much anxious focus we received within that family.

Anxiety focus

Our parents had their own levels of maturity that they brought to family relationships; and their immaturities inevitably get unevenly rationed between each of their children. If you were the child most worried about or focused on in your family, it follows that you'd absorb a bit more of your parents' anxious reactivity than your siblings. The most anxiously focused-on children are more involved in the previous generation's sensitivities and reactions than the less involved siblings.

This is an important factor in understanding how siblings often turn out very differently — an idea that has been explored thoughtfully by Dr Michael Kerr at the Bowen Center.[3]

It isn't really fair is it? We develop our level of solid, mature self through no merit or fault of our own. Some people simply get a better deal than others in terms of the degree of maturity they inherit. At the same time it isn't anyone's fault what level of individual resilience we absorb, and this can help us be compassionate to ourselves and our parents as we learn to accept our immaturities and do our best to patiently lift ourselves a notch higher on the maturity continuum.

Most theories of mental health categorise people into types of illness, with non-symptomatic people deemed to be healthy: you either have a diagnosis or you don't. Bowen theory doesn't see emotional health in terms of illness categories. It views all humans as sitting on a continuum from relatively high differentiation of self, with pretty good functioning, down to low differentiation of self, with collapsed functioning. This means that all of us have the same problem but in different degrees. We all could use more differentiation of self, which means we could all go up a notch in both our ability to keep our emotions and intellect in sync and our ability to stay an individual while present in our relationships.

Confronting the challenge of anxiety and depression

Michael came to counselling with his wife, Shelley, to address the major depression that he had sunk into a month earlier. He'd struggled with debilitating periods of anxiety and feelings of helplessness during earlier periods of his life. His darkest period was his time at university when he had struggled with thoughts of not wanting to live, but meeting Shelley had turned his life around.

Just prior to Michael's slide into depression, he had been the strong one in his marriage. He described how he had supported his wife through her own emotional rollercoaster of dealing with a cancer diagnosis. She had experienced times of feeling overwhelmed during her treatment phase and at times had struggled to leave the house as she grappled with the side effects of chemotherapy and her discomfort relating to people as a cancer patient. While Shelley was struggling, Michael found that he was able to be sturdy for her. He had been aware of his own fears about losing Shelley and his pain in seeing her suffer but mostly he took the role of providing the secure shoulder for Shelley to lean on. As Shelley entered remission she bounced back quickly and threw herself into her busy job in human resources. Michael, however, was not finding it easy to move on. Without Shelley needing him to be strong, his mood had spiralled downward.

Vulnerabilities of self can be switched from one to another in a marriage as circumstances change. Now that Shelley was on her feet again, Michael was struggling to get out of bed each morning. His sleep patterns had deteriorated as he worried incessantly about not meeting his and others' expectations at work. He knew these thoughts were unhelpful but felt unable to switch them off. In order to function at work he had been to his doctor to try antidepressants but was not experiencing much relief from his overwhelming negativity.

Tackling relationship dependence

Michael struggled to correct his exaggerated perfectionist thinking. He could see the mistaken beliefs behind his fears of work failure but beneath these unproductive thoughts was a deeper maturity issue. From a young age, Michael had invested himself and his security in his key positive relationships. He could see that his mood lifted automatically if Shelley needed him to comfort her. It's as if he borrowed resilience from the others' neediness. Michael could see that he avoided any relationship that was not approving and looked to being admired and needed as a way of bypassing his insecurities. Michael and his father had been cut off from each other since his teenage years when his dad had had an affair and left his marriage and family. As well as his pattern of distancing from his father, Michael could see that he developed a heightened sensitivity to his mother's distress levels and strove to be the 'good son' who could bring her happiness. In particular, he had worked hard to gain her pride through academic achievement.

Michael had two ways of reacting in relationships. When he sensed that someone was not approving, he would distance from them and label them as untrustworthy, as he had done with his dad. If he sensed approval from them he would work hard to maintain their admiration, as he had done with his mother. None of this was in Michael's consciousness but could be seen in teasing out the factual story of his relationships. Much of Michael's way of being in the world was in reaction to others. This left him with a low supply of independent functioning to manage when a relationship was not propping him up or when he sensed disapproval.

Being more real rather than feeling better

As Michael came to see the correlation between his dependence on relationships and his sense of wellbeing, he could shift his focus from trying to fix his symptoms to trying to grow himself up. This growing-up process was going to need to be taken one step at a time as the wiring to react to others was deeply ingrained. When he had focused on how badly he felt, how anxious he was, and how hard it was to sleep, he found that he would become increasingly overwhelmed. His symptom focus left him feeling helpless and looking to the 'experts' to come up with a solution. However, when Michael started to work on himself and not his symptoms, he took his focus off his feelings and started to work on his day-to-day adult responsibilities, such as getting to bed at a reasonable hour, eating three meals a day, doing daily light exercise and getting himself to work on time. These efforts were focused on using his inner resources at a basic level rather than looking to others to motivate him with praise and encouragement.

Prior to tackling his own self-management, Michael had fallen into a pattern of allowing Shelley to treat him as the patient. He was letting her manage all his appointments, as well as allowing her to remind him to take his medication and cook and clean up for him. Shelley talked through how she could return to treating Michael as her husband and not be a caretaker for him. This meant she started asking for his help again and shared with him her own daily ups and downs. She worked to even up the lopsided relationship rather than to focus on trying to fix Michael.

As Michael worked to better understand himself in his family he began to consider ways he could make contact with his father and begin to get to know him as a person rather than continue to write him off as a villain. None of these efforts was easy for Michael and his progress in managing himself and staying in contact with others was often slow. His anxieties about letting people down at work, and his consequent drain in energy and sleep disruption, were also slow to improve. Michael did, however, report feeling stronger as a person, with a growing acceptance of the sensitivities generated in his earlier relationships.

I recall Michael speaking about the struggle to accept how hard it was to function without lots of approval.

At times I get so discouraged with how consumed I get with my awful thoughts. I can see that both Mum and Dad, in different ways, struggled with their confidence and looked to others to boost them. I guess it isn't any wonder that I struggle as well. I wish I had been given a better deal from my family patterns but I get that I have to do the best I can with what I've got.

For Michael, and others like him who struggle with disproportionate fears and discouragements, it's helpful to take the focus off feelings and to look at doing things that strengthen maturity from within. Following are three guidelines that can assist with this in the midst of challenging symptoms.

1. Function rather than fix

Look at the things you can manage to do each day that keep you responsible for yourself. When life energy is at a low ebb this might not be much more than feeding yourself three decent meals and getting out of bed when the alarm goes off.

2. Be a person rather than a patient

Take care not to allow others to take over basic responsibilities for you. Even when receiving medical advice stay involved in your choices and keep managing your own diary.

3. Keep in contact with others

The easiest thing to do when the pressure is high is to avoid others, especially those who are most challenging to your confidence. The more you are able to maintain some contact with a variety of people, the more you are able to experience yourself as a solid person.

You can see that the focus is on taking small, realistic steps to be more of a self. It isn't the same as a purely medical approach to mental illness which focuses on fixing the symptoms. Rather than analyse the severity of symptoms, the premise is that when a person can lift their functioning just a tad, their symptoms start to become less overwhelming.

Keep putting one foot in front of the other

To grow up in the face of the energy drain of anxiety and depression can be an enormous challenge. The most important principle is to not give up your responsibility for managing yourself to the best of your current ability, no matter how compromised this may be. The more you fall into becoming a patient, who is dependent on others and medication to solve the problem, the more you contribute to an increase in helplessness. This doesn't mean medication isn't sometimes a helpful choice but it should not be at the expense of working on managing yourself in the basic responsibilities of each day. And if you can see that a family member is taking on the role of managing your condition, it's timely for you to step up and get back in charge of your own health care. This is not easy when you feel so lacking in personal resources but it will assist you to hold onto enough adult self to be able to keep moving forward wisely and compassionately.

Sensitivity to relationships impacts our maturity

One of Michael's challenges was accepting that he could not grow up quickly beyond the amount of maturity available to him from his family patterns. With maturity levels sitting on a continuum, from very low to moderately high, each of us is working from a different starting point in our efforts to grow up. As earlier chapters of this book have described, we all leave our childhoods with degrees of sensitivity to how others perceive us. The more highly tuned this relationship sensitivity is, the more anxiously we will live our lives. When we try to imagine what others think of us in terms of disapproval or rejection, the more we use up our life energy in relationships. If our efforts go into looking for threats of disapproval from others, the more difficult it will be to have boundaries that enable us to work on strengthening our inner self.

Realising that we all start at different levels of maturity, through no fault of our own and similarly through no fault of our parents, helps us to have some compassion for our own and others' slow progress in growing up. When there is a less solid self in relationships a person is much more vulnerable to times of feeling overwhelmed and directionless. Life's stressors start to take an increased toll on their health and moods, and emotional symptoms start to come to the surface.

It's helpful to remember that the degree to which a person relies on relationships to steady themselves can be connected to their level of maturity and may play a part in their vulnerability to developing anxiety and mood symptoms.

Examples of types of relationship dependency

So what are the different ways that dependency on relationships can drain our capacity to cope with life's stresses? Here are a few examples:

> » If a person depends on others to calm things down when they are fearful, they are likely to struggle to draw on their internal resources to stay on track in the face of challenges.

» If a person relies on validation to be able to get a job done well, they are prone to dropping their performance levels when there is a hint of criticism or when no one is there to approve of their work.

» If a person is accustomed to being a helper and gains their sense of resilience from this role, they may be prone to collapsing when they are no longer needed or appreciated as the advisor and reliable one.

» If a person has invested intensely in a relationship as a substitute for past disappointing relationships, they can be destabilised easily and feel empty when the relationship hits a bumpy patch.

In anxious times we each have different degrees of relationship patterns that we fall into to get some relief from stress. At the same time, the extent to which we use these patterns determines the extent that we are vulnerable to losing our balance. The key stress-relieving patterns that are a potential hazard to emotional health are:

» too much distance;

» doing too much for another;

» allowing others to do what is responsibly ours to do.

It is useful to consider how much you use these patterns if you want to improve your mental health and build more resilience to deal with life stress. And remember that every pattern is fuelled by both sides of a relationship. While change only requires one person to change their part, there are always counteractions to contend with while travelling the path of positive change.

Dealing with unfairness without becoming a martyr

Another uneven playing field for our growing up is the degree of life tragedy that different people are faced with. This is another part of life that can seem unfair. There are many who face challenges that are well beyond the expected life stressors. Life seems to deal out very different levels of pain that can leave people feeling overwhelmed with the burden of just surviving each day. Finding maturity for such testing circumstances, such as the death of a child, chronic illness or having to care for a severely disabled family member, is the most daunting of challenges. When traumatic events occur, it is completely understandable that just getting through each day is an achievement in maturity.

Yet it's also the case that many people speak of how trials have helped increase their resilience and inner wisdom. People who have come through suffering without bitterness and have regained a meaningful life are often looked to as the wisest in society.

A common maturity trap for a person facing ongoing pressures on their coping resources is to become overly immersed in the hardship. Much of this book speaks of finding the balance between caring about others and responsibly caring for yourself. If either end of this spectrum is exaggerated, the result is an unhealthy self-absorption or other absorption that narrows the experience of life. Large disappointments are bound to create a period of pervasive grief and loss but a person's growing up is compromised if they fall into the trap of making a life project out of the disappointment that has occurred. People who immerse themselves in the circumstances of grief are often experienced by others as living a martyr role of sacrificing all personal interest.

A story of making a project out of grief

Cheryl had struggled to find a balance in responding to the severe disability of her fourth child, Lucy. In her younger years she had always felt responsible for her father's wellbeing after he had suffered a life-threatening heart attack and her mother had seemed unable to cope on her own. When her baby daughter was diagnosed with cystic fibrosis, Cheryl struggled with the understandable contradictions of grief: sadness, denial, anger and guilt. Having been so programmed to make things right for others, she set out to do whatever it took to give her daughter a rich and satisfying life.

In many ways it was admirable that Cheryl found a way to get beyond shock and grief to making the best of Lucy's circumstances. This, however, had grown into such a focus that her prime topic of conversation with her husband and friends was Lucy's needs. Cheryl went to every program available to educate herself about Lucy's condition and became actively involved in lobbying for improved respite care and support for families caring for a disabled child. Such helpful efforts were becoming a stumbling block to Cheryl's growth as her absorption in helping Lucy contributed to her increasing isolation from her family and friends.

Considering your part in resentment build-up

I met Cheryl and her husband, Barry, when Lucy was nine years old. Cheryl poured out a barrage of resentment about the load that had fallen on her shoulders in caring for Lucy. She spoke with a sarcastic tone about Barry and her other teenage children living 'the good life' while she bore the brunt of Lucy's increasing medical demands. I felt deeply for what Cheryl had been confronted with and how much it had interrupted the life course she had anticipated. The sticking point for Cheryl, however, was that she couldn't see outside her resentments; she felt sorry for herself but had not stopped to reflect on how she had inadvertently contributed to her own bitterness.

In describing her story of caring for Lucy, Cheryl began to realise that she had anxiously taken on all the responsibility for her daughter's life without addressing her own emotional wellbeing or staying connected to others. Of course, Cheryl's husband Barry was complicit in this pattern by keeping his distance from his wife. Barry had not developed or expressed his own views to Cheryl about the role he would like in parenting Lucy and had not taken the initiative to maintain the connection he wanted in his marriage.

The key challenge that Cheryl confronted was to shift from trying to get Barry and others to see how much she had sacrificed as her way of regaining some strength. In working out how she could reclaim some of herself, Cheryl started to consider how much she could do for Lucy without neglecting the other important parts of her life. A helpful realisation in this journey was that, as Cheryl learnt not to drop everything to attend to the first sign of Lucy's distress, she noticed a gradual reduction in Lucy's demanding behaviour.

Cheryl was facing a life challenge that would set anyone back in their life management. She was, however, able to take the critical first step to reigniting her growth in maturity. She started examining her own part in her difficulties. She could not change Lucy's diagnosis, but she could change the way she was reacting to it. Cheryl found enough maturity in her inner storehouse to work on what was within her control to reduce her own sense of entrapment.

Staying realistic and compassionate

Having a realistic view of the obstacles ahead of you is vital to making progress in growing up. It is not helpful to compare yourself to others who may have inherited more differentiation or who have not had as many challenges as you have had to deal with. The key is to have an awareness of your levels of maturity and current capacity to manage yourself outside of depending on others. From here you can see the next level of growing up that is going to lift your resilience a notch.

The principles of focusing on yourself and not changing others are the same maturity ingredients for us all: drawing on your own wisdom rather than looking to others to direct you. However, the step to improving your self-direction will look different dependent on where your current point of growth is and how many traumas have come your way. If you are highly sensitive to others' approval, and have also had some extraordinary setbacks, then progress will be in small steps of looking after yourself. If you are fortunate in starting from a less anxious place, you can work from a different level. No matter what starting point of maturity you are working from, the goal is the same: to work on yourself responsibly, to clarify your principles and to connect with others less reactively.

Questions for reflection

» What evidence is there for seeing maturity as a continuum that is inherited from generational relationships? How does this help me to be realistic about my and others' growing-up efforts?

» To what degree do I use relationships to steady myself? How does this guide me in understanding my level of maturity?

» When I am faced with setbacks in coping with life, how can I apply the principles to:

a) function (manage routine) rather than fix (make symptoms go away);

b) stay a person (responsible for what I can manage) rather than become a patient (letting others manage me);

c) keep contact (initiate connection times) rather than cut off (avoid others)?

It may be helpful when considering these questions to refer to Appendix 4 for more information on differentiation of self.

part 5

MATURITY
enhancement
in *the* SECOND HALF
of life

Midlife

Crisis or an opportunity for growth?

[Crises can be averted] 'when one can find a [person] with the courage to define self, who is as invested in the welfare of the family as in self, who is neither angry nor dogmatic, whose energy goes to changing self rather than telling others what they should do.'[1]

—Murray Bowen MD

'We would all like to be ourselves in our families, to have them accept us for who we really are. But we may lose sight of the prerequisite; that we accept *them* for who they really are, getting past the anger resentments, and regrets of not being a family like the Brady Bunch.'[2]

—Monica McGoldrick PhD

Is there really such a thing as a midlife crisis? Why is it that some seem comfortable to accept that their youth is behind them while others seem to experience their ageing as a catastrophe? There's no doubt that moving into the second half of life confronts us with our mortality. We realise that many of the expectations we took for granted during our more naively optimistic younger years have not been realised. It's common to feel disappointed at family life not having measured up to the hopes and expectations of earlier years. Just the other day in my office I listened as a 50-year-old male clearly summed up the potential midlife challenge. He declared, 'I can't remember feeling this insecure since my adolescence. My career is in a stalemate, my marriage of twenty years is in flux, my kids don't need me anymore; and on top of all that my running days are over because of my dicky knees! I feel like everything's downhill from here!'

When things in life don't seem to be fulfilling our dreams we are all prone to slipping back into childish protests. Remember the hallmarks of a child's responses to frustrations mentioned in the opening chapter? The infant's feelings rule their behaviour and they struggle to tolerate any delay in getting what they want. Their world is geared around self-gratification. They tend to act on impulse to satisfy their yearnings and to lose their temper with whoever stands in their way. Can you see how these immaturities might come to the fore when the middle phase of life is disappointing us?

The growing-up challenge is to not dwell solely on the disappointments and losses of life, but rather to think through how we want to deal with these setbacks. It is at the challenging times of life that a bit of maturity can be the difference between riding the setback wave or being swamped by it. Here's a reminder of the maturity traits that enable us to negotiate our way through disappointments without catastrophising all aspects of our lives. We make a conscious effort to bring our feelings in line with our intellect and we practise staying steady while not having our wants immediately met; our attention focuses on developing our inner principles rather than criticising others; when people disagree with us we're able to stay connected; we stay responsible for solving our own problems and do not crowd others' space so that they can find their own way through their problems; we don't shift our viewpoint in order to fit in with the group; and we're able to see beyond ourselves to the bigger picture of reactions and counter-reactions.

How midlife can expose our maturity gaps

Changes and losses in midlife can expose where we have avoided areas of responsible growth. Many marriages fall on shaky ground in midlife, as each spouse realises that differences between them and their partner have gone unaddressed and instead have been channelled into work or the children. When this occurs, there is bound to be a crisis when the children leave home or when work no longer provides the validation and status it once did.

Laura and Gavin were caught by surprise by such a crisis as they entered midlife. Both were in their late forties, with four children ranging from age fourteen to 21. Gavin had invested huge amounts of time in his business role and Laura had immersed herself in the activities of their children. Laura relished her role as a mother and was actively involved in her children's community activities. She had made a strong network of friends through the children and regularly organised social events, in which Gavin happily participated. Gavin had always tried to be an involved father on weekends and attended his children's sport if he was not on a business trip. He was proud of his children but had become accustomed to Laura keeping him in the loop about their lives. This meant that Gavin had gradually stopped making an effort to have a separate, one-on-one relationship with his daughter and three sons.

On the surface all seemed well for Laura and Gavin. They did not fight and they enjoyed attending Gavin's business functions together and events connected to Laura's volunteer work at school.

As a couple, however, they had stopped spending any exclusive time together where they could share their own joys, fears and doubts. Twenty years ago this would have been unthinkable to them both, as they knew each other's ups and downs so well. They continued a fairly routine sex life and did not complain about how life was going. Financially Gavin had done very well and they enjoyed a life of relative affluence.

The crisis of a midlife affair

When Gavin and Laura came to counselling, Laura had just discovered that Gavin was having an affair with Clare, a woman he had met through work. They were both devastated to find themselves and their marriage in such a crisis. Gavin was clear that he had not gone looking for the affair. He described that when he had met Clare, he was taken aback by how much interest she had in his work and how she could offer him great insights into his business dilemmas. It was only after the start of the affair that Gavin realised how much he had missed Laura being interested in his business life.

The strength of the attraction Gavin experienced caught him by surprise. The relationship with Clare had remained at a friendship level for some months but started to intensify as Gavin started to vent to Clare about feeling lonely in his marriage. Then the secrecy and deception started as the emotional affair moved into the sexual realm.

Laura was understandably shocked and angry at the betrayal she felt. 'I have always been so confident that our marriage was rock solid,' she explained. 'We never have disagreements and we have made such a good team together in terms of raising a family and setting up a good lifestyle. I just could not see this coming — it's hit me like a steam train!'

Gavin stated:

> To be honest, I didn't feel unhappy in my marriage when I met
> Clare. I'm not about to make excuses for what I've done. It's
> all been devastating for Laura, and also for Clare. When Clare
> took an interest in my work issues, I can see that it opened
> up the extent of the gap that had developed in my life with
> Laura. I was quite insecure about work at the time but I wasn't
> acknowledging that to myself. When the friendship with Clare
> developed I started to think that Laura had been neglecting me.
> This was so unfair on Laura because I hadn't even let her know
> about what was happening for me at work. I have to also admit
> that I misled Clare by telling her how unhappy my marriage was.

As both Gavin and Laura confronted the crisis of the affair, they saw
it as a giant wake-up call. In spite of all the anger and confusion, both
of them believed they had a good marriage and were prepared to try
to work things out. As they examined their lives to date, it became
clear to both Gavin and Laura how much their marriage had been
neglected. Neither had taken the time to think through how they were
living their lives. It would have been easy for Gavin to blame Laura
for her disinterest in his work, but he could acknowledge how he
had allowed this to happen and had stopped taking an interest in
Laura's activities or sharing his projects with her. Laura admitted that
her emotional intimacy needs had unknowingly transferred to her
children and Gavin could see that his sense of importance was tied
up with work success. As Gavin had entered his forties he had lost
some confidence as younger executives had moved ahead of him in
the organisation. This had left him even more vulnerable to attaching
to someone who could affirm his identity at work.

Laura and Gavin's neglect of their marriage had been compounded by the demands of elderly parents. Gavin's mother had recently moved to a nursing home. Laura, as a dependable eldest daughter, had been the primary visitor to her mother-in-law as well as the one who shouldered most of the responsibility for her own parents' medical needs. Taking on this responsibility on top of parenting had left Laura with little remaining energy for her marriage. She believed that looking after Gavin's mother was her way of caring for Gavin, but ultimately it was adding to the breach in their connection with each other.

The challenges that Gavin and Laura were facing in midlife are all too common. Gavin and Laura did manage to get their marriage back on track but not without great pain and heartache for all involved. With the intensity of strong emotions that overwhelm people when an affair is uncovered, it is not surprising that many couples are not able to find their way back to addressing neglected intimacy issues in their marriages.

Losing the security props of youth

Once midlife is reached, the external supports that may have built superficial self-confidence earlier in life have been diminished. Such props may include physical attractiveness, relationship validation and career success. The growing-up challenge at this time is to decide whether to seek replacement external props, such as affairs and new toys, or to find ways of steadying yourself that don't rely on externals. Midlife is a bit like the half-time break in a football game: it provides the opportunity to step back and look at how you are playing the game and whether some adjustments in approach need to be made. There is a valuable opportunity to ask many self-reflection questions such as:

- » Which relationships are my priorities?
- » What important relationships have I been neglecting?
- » Where have I lost my balance in terms of investing my life energies?
- » What is my own job description as a spouse, as a daughter/son, as a friend, as a worker?
- » Am I going to let the external circumstances of life direct me or will I grow the strength of my inner thinking guidance system?

As I write this chapter, I am travelling through the midlife years with the joys of menopause symptoms, needing two pairs of glasses for driving and reading, and coping with a shoulder strain from trying to maintain my previous capacity to carry ten shopping bags at once. I am adjusting to an empty nest, with my daughters establishing themselves as independent adults. I can see how much I have invested in my role as a parent and can see the areas of my marriage that need some attention. I can also see that the deeper questions of life meaning should not be neglected.

The challenges of mid and later life reveal to us that the experiences of years alone don't automatically mature us. We won't grow up much if we live from decade to decade seeking to shore ourselves up with validating relationships and without ever examining our own life. With the pace of modern life intensifying, it is particularly difficult to find the space and energy to do such re-visioning. Often it takes a crisis to motivate us to make this a priority.

I have heard many people express a sense of grief and regret that they had not learnt about genuine growing up when they were younger. 'If only I had known these things before I had children! Or before I left my husband! Or before my child moved away! Or before my father died! Or before I confronted my sister!'

Dealing with regrets is tough. We run the risk of either being overly harsh on ourselves or blaming others so we avoid facing our own vulnerabilities. The growing-up alternative is to take time to understand the patterns we have fallen into and to determine how we can begin to relate with a little bit more thoughtful awareness. Small shifts in relating responsibly can have profound ripple effects for both ourselves and those dear to us.

Questions for reflection

» Think of how you responded to a recent life disappointment. How has your reaction exposed childish protests and how has it revealed mature self-examination?
» What priorities have you unintentionally been neglecting in the business of life?
» Are there aspects of your behaviour in relationships that need attention if they're going to be secure when other props fall away?

14.

Ageing well

Retirement, the empty nest, relating to a third generation

'There are also those who kid themselves into believing they have "worked out" the relationship with parents and who make brief formal visits home without personal communication; they use as evidence of maturity that they do not see their parents.'[1]

—Murray Bowen MD

'A person's level of differentiation [maturity] can best be observed in an anxious family setting.'[2]

—Daniel Papero PhD

With huge improvements in health care our life expectancy is increasing. This means that older age can be a substantial part of our life cycle that we would do well to be thoughtful about. The life changes we face as older adults are significant and can bring our maturity gaps to the fore. This is the time when children are making their way in their own families. Sons- and daughters-in-law come onto the scene of our family systems. Grandchildren come along.

Retirement can dramatically change the rhythm of each day and the amount of time that spouses now spend sharing each other's space. Health scares become more common and confront us with our mortality. Any phase of life that changes the predictable pattern of contact in relationships provides an excellent opportunity to work on being a more real self. As older age strips away contact with some of the relationships that have helped us to feel more secure, we have the chance to build more surety from the inside out.

Life after retirement

Malcolm was looking forward to retirement now that he was approaching 60. Having started his own business 40 years ago he had managed to find a buyer and was pleased with the financial security this would give him and his wife Julia. They could now turn their attention to considering travel opportunities and options for downsizing from the family home where they'd raised their four children. All but one of their children had successfully established themselves in their careers and in steady relationships. Their youngest son, Andrew, still spent time living at home when his jobs fell through and he'd become depressed, but Julia had stuck by him and was doing all she could to help him lift off.

Some months into this new chapter of life Malcolm was feeling completely lost. He had lots of plans for exploring real estate options, working on his golf and getting involved in a community charity, but he found he had no energy to take the initiative in any of these ventures. With his life at an impasse he turned to Julia to help him. Julia was always one to help others and she was eager to give Malcolm advice about how to give his retirement some structure and satisfaction. Malcolm was grateful for her ideas but as the weeks rolled on and his energy levels remained depleted, Julia started to get short with him. She began to get busier with her own activities and spent little time at home. Malcolm didn't know what to do with each day. He had tried to spend more time helping Andrew at Julia's prompting but Andrew seemed unreachable to him and unwilling to listen to his career advice.

When too much energy goes into one area

Malcolm's adjustment difficulties are not uncommon. Much of his life energy over the past decades had been invested in his work. This had helped him to feel more stable in his marriage as it gave him distance from the intensity he felt from Julia's expectations of him and it seemed to calm Julia down as he secured some financial stability for them. Julia, on the other hand, had invested most of her life energy into raising the children. The more the children seemed to need her, the less she seemed to need from her marriage. As the youngest child, Andrew, hit a difficult patch in late adolescence, Julia had increased her efforts to help Andrew to feel better about himself.

While there's nothing wrong with putting creative life energy into work and child rearing, this becomes a problem when it's done as an alternative to growing more real in a marriage. Malcolm had invested more of himself in his work over the years as it had enabled him to avoid figuring out what his response would be to Julia's requests for him to back her up with Andrew. Julia had invested more of her thinking and planning time in her children's lives than in her own. This had felt comfortable to her as it enabled her to steer clear of the tension she felt early in her marriage about helping out with earning income. When work and children become substitutes for addressing our own insecurities and any unspoken ideals about how we will be in our marriage, our lives are bound to feel shaky when these substitutes are no longer there in the same way.

Triangle detours and different functional positions had helped to keep things stable for Malcolm and Julia over many years but retirement had upset this balance, leaving Malcolm with an increasingly depressed mood and Julia increasingly dissatisfied with her marriage. Malcolm had used work as his triangle detour from the tension about meeting Julia's expectations of him as a father. Julia had triangled her children into being her main satisfactions in life who provided her with a sense of value that she had struggled to find in her marriage. Malcolm was over-functioning at work and in managing the family finances with Julia not interested in being involved. Julia had over-functioned in managing the relationships at home with Malcolm slipping into minimal involvement in managing their domestic, parenting and social lives. What had been adaptive at one phase of their lives was no longer a pattern that could keep things stable.

Malcolm realised that the main project for adjusting to ageing was to be in better contact with his wife, his children and his extended family. He would need to work on not depending on Julia to sort his life out but to become interested in her as a person. He reported that his biggest challenge was learning not to shy away from expressing a disagreement with Julia but to be clear about his opinion on what he wasn't willing to go along with. Malcolm had let his relationship with his own siblings and elderly parents be neglected over many years. Julia and his parents had had a falling out when their first child was born and he had backed away from his family to keep the peace in his marriage. This cut-off from his broader family had left Malcolm too dependent on too few people, which was putting an increasing strain on his current family relationships. As Malcolm began to take small steps to reconnect with his family of origin he noticed the pressure reduce when he was with Julia. Julia was supportive of his efforts to see his parents as long as he wasn't asking her to do the work for him with his own family.

Malcolm summed up his lessons from adjusting to his retirement by saying:

> I thought my problem would be solved by finding more activities to fill up my time, but what I really needed to do was learn how to relate again to the most influential people in my life. I didn't need more external projects as distractions; I needed to be more of a real person to my wife, my kids and my parents.

The empty nest and a new generation

I'd always thought that having my children leave home and be responsible for their own lives would be a time for rejoicing, a time to reclaim some space for life projects that had, of necessity, been shelved years ago, and a time to enjoy being just a couple again after all these years. In many ways this has been so, but the challenges of entering this phase have caught me by surprise. I wasn't prepared for how much I had become accustomed to having a strong influence in my daughters' lives. When they had been at home I could indirectly have some shared responsibility in their lives by determining what food was in the refrigerator and having a voice over many dinners about relationship and career dilemmas. Until they left home I hadn't realised how much I was still functioning for them.

It's been another step of growing up for me to work to reduce the merging of boundaries or the fusion that I still have with my grown daughters. When one of my daughters still invites this type of relating through her upsets, it's been especially hard to keep my own counsel about staying in my own skin and not propping her up. I've seen how much better she's able to manage her emotions when I don't step in to try to do it for her. My other daughter has been less overt in asking for support from me but I've still found myself concerned about how she's managing with looking after herself. When I worry about them I don't relate to them in a real way, where I can be a resource to them as opposed to setting up subtle roadblocks to their own maturing. I'm learning to take an interest in their lives without trying to advise or influence them. This doesn't come naturally to me but I can see the improvement in our adult relationships as I work on these boundaries. I also see that this makes it much easier for my son-in-law to find his space in our family system where his wife (my daughter) is less caught between the attachments of one generation to the next.

And there's no point working on adjusting to the empty nest by just addressing my relationship with my daughters. My marriage is my main attachment and the one that absorbs most of my anxieties. This is the place I need to work at being real as I learn how to age gracefully. My own litmus test for being real in my marriage is that if I become irritated with my husband I'm not being an honest self to him and others. Being more mature in my marriage means consciously being in close contact with David, expressing both the positives and negatives from my own position — not absorbing his upsets for him or telling him how I think he should be.

Grandparenting: beware of skipping a generation

Helen had awaited the birth of her first grandchild with excited anticipation. She had begun shopping for baby items and imagining holding this little piece of her own genetic make-up in her arms. Life was going to change for Helen. She had reduced her work hours and looked forward to being an active grandmother who looked after her son's child a few times a week. She wondered what the child would be called — would her name be in there somehow? Would this little one call her Nanna or Gran?

When I first met Helen she reported that her life was falling apart. Her grandson was nearly one and she barely got to see him. Her son, Aaron, would bring him for short visits but not leave him with her. Her daughter-in-law, Sarah, was not speaking with her and had given the impression that Helen wasn't welcome to visit. What had gone so wrong at a life transition full of so many positive dreams?

I asked Helen about how she saw the problem that meant she wasn't feeling like she could be a grandmother. 'It's all Sarah's fault,' she said. 'She's so possessive and controlling of Aaron and is taking away my rights as a grandmother. I tell Aaron that it's just not acceptable. My life feels like it's been ruined by this awful girl.'

As Helen sobbed in my office I wondered how to help her think her way out from this hurt and blaming position. I asked her about her relationship with her son since he had married. How often had they had contact and what kind of things had they shared with each other? 'Aaron has seemed distant to me for years now,' Helen answered. 'He's been very dutiful in visiting me but he doesn't let me in on what's happening in his life. He didn't tell me about his relationship with Sarah until he'd already proposed to her.'

I asked what Helen's response was to the news of his marriage. She replied, 'I was thrilled about the marriage. I'd worried that he was leaving things too late to settle down and start a family of his own. My first thoughts were that finally my son was going to give me grandchildren. I've looked forward to this moment for all my life.'

Helen's responses revealed that she had put all of her focus on her relationship with her grandchild and had stopped working on having an adult relationship with her son. Clearly Aaron had not made it easy for her by keeping a dutiful but distant relationship, but

Helen had certainly played her part in this superficial relationship. Rather than working at being interested in Aaron's life as opposed to pursuing him, Helen had put all of her relationship energy into planning for grandparenting. It isn't surprising that the intensity of these expectations, combined with the distance between mother and son, led to an upset between Helen and her daughter-in-law Sarah.

Initially Helen wanted to get Sarah to come to counselling so that she could be 'sorted out'. But as she began to see how Sarah had become caught in a triangle because of what had not been addressed between herself and her son, Helen decided to invite Aaron to come to a session to talk things through. Aaron was keen to get some help as he was feeling like the meat in the sandwich between his wife and his mother. He acknowledged that he had been more focused on keeping the peace with both these important women in his life than in defining his own views to them. Helen's efforts went onto shifting her focus away from her grandson and back to her own son. She could see how much she'd assumed about her role as grandmother without asking Aaron what he thought. Helen also could see that she had put too many relationship eggs into one basket and needed to invest some energy in her broader network of friends and family. One of her biggest challenges was to stop using her friends as allies to take her side against her daughter-in-law. This triangle detour had helped her to temporarily feel better but had certainly not helped her to address her own part in the difficulties.

Gaining strength from within ourselves

At any phase of life our immaturities can be assessed by asking ourselves how much we gain strength through being needed by others or through knowing ourselves and being steadied by our principles. How much do we use children, grandchildren or work to steady us instead of taking responsibility for our own growth? The more we have relied on being needed and affirmed by others, the more prone we may be to eliciting over-helping from others when infirmities begin to appear. To navigate a steady course through the potentially long period of ageing in our lives it is worth reflecting on the degree to which we rely on others to make us feel needed. Addressing this question can mean the difference between ageing with inner direction versus ageing with dissolution.

Questions for reflection

» How much life energy have I put into relationships or pursuits that reduce or end during later life? Am I thinking about how to be present in my more neglected important relationships during my advanced years?

» To what degree have I relied on being important in my children's lives? Can I learn to steady myself using my principles rather than through being needed or attended to?

» When I think about relating to grandchildren, do I override the importance of working on my relationship with my son or daughter?

» In what ways can I be more present in my marriage as an older person, even when it involves confronting difficulties honestly?

15.

Old age and facing death
Denial or honest preparation

'Chief among all taboo subjects is death. A high percentage of people die alone, locked into their own thoughts which they cannot communicate to others.'[1]

—Murray Bowen MD

'Families facing death must adjust to more than the loss of a loved one. The fundamental reorganisation resonates with the history of previous generations and will resound into generations yet to come.'[2]

—Elliott Rosen ED

The most painful time in my life to date was the death of my mother to breast cancer when she was just 54 years old. Her untimely loss was heart wrenching, but alongside her painful death there is another level of sadness for me. This is the layer of how her death was handled in our family. I remember being in denial about her imminent death right up to her last ambulance ride to hospital. None of our family talked about her dying and how we were going to support each other.

My mother kept up a courageous presence and spoke of future plans. My father went on a planned trip to a sporting event with his male friends a fortnight before she died. All of us were using distance to cope with what was too painful to confront. We just shut out the facts and the aching emotions in order to keep moving forward. Well-meaning friends made efforts to talk with me about my mother's deteriorating condition and the prospect of her death being near but I didn't want any part in such pessimistic conversation.

Shutting down feelings in order to move on

When I look at the generations of my mother's and father's families, I can see that this stoic way of dealing with death goes back a long way. Children were not included in funerals, adults did not show their distress in front of others and normal routines were resumed as soon as the funeral was over. This pattern of moving on without dwelling on loss has helped the family to survive in many ways. When my dad's father died suddenly at the age of 50 of a heart attack, it was vital for my father to quickly take the reins of the family business to prevent financial ruin for himself and his mother. Having just come through the Great Depression, financial survival took precedence over dealing with personal pain. Similarly, when my mother's eldest brother died as a young child, the whole society was rebuilding from the loss of a generation of young men in World War I. People had to find a way to move on without falling into despair or having their livelihoods collapse.

Moving so far in the direction of shutting off feelings to survive has had its cost. I regret that I could never talk to my mother about what she was going through. It would have helped to have been able to cry together. The family could have been a supportive resource if individuals were able to balance their efforts to keep going with time to talk with each other about our struggles in the midst of grief. Thirty years later I can still awaken the deep hurt and helplessness that I felt after Mum's death, hearing my father crying in his bed at night and calling out my mother's name. I knew how to support him through busily helping with tasks but I had no idea how to talk to him about our shared loss. The shockwave of my mother's death and the limits to being able to grieve openly were evident in my family for a long while. Some family members went through some significant emotional symptoms and there are still traces of anger and blame from this time.

Keeping the balance — Gloria's story

As with each phase of the life cycle, the core to maturity is to find a balance between being connected and being independent. When facing death this is especially important so that there is opportunity to share grief together as well as the space to find a way to keep coping with life's responsibilities. My family were a long way down the separateness end of the continuum. It was as if we had an in-built instinct in the face of illness and death to avoid the sensitive topics and become closed in our communication. Other families, in contrast, become so absorbed in the feelings of loss that they are unable to move forward and may spend years maintaining the memory of their loved one at the expense of their own life tasks.

Does anyone get close to this maturity balance when facing the end of life? There are many brave people who have chosen to work on dealing with death in as helpful a way as possible. One such courageous person was 78-year-old Gloria. Gloria came to see me when she was diagnosed with cancer. She had just had surgery but there were some secondary cancers that had not been removed. Gloria had not given up hope of a remission and was putting as much energy as she could into her follow-up treatments. She was also attending relaxation classes and watching her diet closely. Gloria's main concern, however, was that if she were to die soon she knew she hadn't brought the best that she could to her important relationships. I recall her saying: 'I probably don't have much time left and I know I have some things to work on in my family if I'm going to say goodbye properly.'

It's not too late to review how we relate

Gloria understood that facing death is not just something for the individual but presents a pivotal life event for all who are significant to the dying person. She was committed to the challenge of growing up at the end of her life by not focusing on how others in her family were going to cope with her illness. Instead she wanted to look at what she could do differently to help relationships be as open and connected as possible.

The first relationship Gloria considered was her marriage of over 50 years. She acknowledged that she had grown distant with Bill and that they were just co-existing. Their marriage was peaceful but Gloria saw that in many ways they were living parallel lives. Gloria reflected on her own experience of this disconnect at a time in life when she was experiencing lots of fears and vulnerability. She had been the one in the relationship to direct family proceedings and organise her husband to fit in. Bill had readily accepted her taking over for him in this way. Gloria acknowledged how lonely she was with this arrangement. She reflected on the many years of sleeping in separate beds and thought about how much she missed some human touch and the comfort of another's body warmth in bed at night. 'It just happened gradually over time,' she explained. 'Now that I stop to think of it, I am really lonely and I am guessing Bill is as well. He's never been one to complain though, always just going along with things.'

Gloria planned how she would use her own initiative to move towards Bill. They had planned a holiday following her current course of treatment. Gloria determined that she would work on doing two things while she was away. Firstly, she would express her fears to Bill and say how much she needed him to be alongside her. Secondly, she would start snuggling up to him in bed and not worry about his reactions. After her holiday, Gloria reported that both efforts had brought her tremendous relief and she and Bill were enjoying more affection than they had for decades. She was starting to experience Bill differently — less as a dependent and more as an equal who could share the load of coping with life, and death.

Gloria spent a good deal of time reflecting on the patterns of her own parents' marriage and how she had viewed her mother as the strong and critical one and her father as the weaker 'hen-pecked' husband. She realised that she and Bill had replicated a similar pattern. This also helped her to get a broader perspective on her relationship with her daughters, particularly her younger daughter, Bronwyn, who seemed uncomfortably cold when they were together. She could see that Bronwyn had been more her father's support and that this would have affected her view of her mother, just as it had for Gloria with her own mother. She stopped herself from trying so hard to pursue Bronwyn and instead started to focus on being more interested in the goings-on of her grandchildren. Gloria could see that the more anxiety she felt about the distance in her relationship with her younger daughter, the tenser she was in her presence. Focusing on the grandchildren was a way of taking out the intensity from their interactions.

Gloria could chat about the most recent school concert as a way to break the ice with her daughter. As they started to relax more around each other, Gloria was able to share a bit more about her own life with Bronwyn. In turn Bronwyn began to open up just a little, about her own challenges juggling children and career. Gloria's oldest grandchild was preparing for his thirteenth birthday party and she was thrilled when Bronwyn asked her to be involved in some of the catering for the celebration.

Getting out of the old family triangle

Gloria made a conscious effort to demonstrate to both her daughters her loving commitment to their father and her appreciation for the strength and support he was showing her. In this way she was changing her old habit of triangling her daughters into her marriage frustrations. She was aware of how many times she had spoken in demeaning ways about Bill to her daughters and how awkward this triangle behaviour would be for them. Gloria asked both of her daughters to come to her treatments with her on a couple of occasions. She expressed to them how much she valued their presence as it helped her to feel less alone in the face of her fear about going through the process of dying.

Gloria had a good six-month period of reasonable health following her course of chemotherapy and she was able to work on being both real and warm in all her key relationships with rewarding results. There was still some caution from Bronwyn about opening up too much to her mother but they had made progress in being able to enjoy the children together. When Gloria received bad news that the cancer had spread further, she spoke at length to Bill about whether to have another bout of chemo. Together they decided that continuing to enjoy the improved quality of their marriage was more important than trying to buy a bit more time and suffer the terrible fatigue and nausea that came with the treatment. Gloria reflected on how different this was to her previous way of coping, where she would ask the doctors to go ahead and do whatever they could without talking about the implications to Bill.

Gloria met with each of her daughters separately to tell them the news and what she had decided to do with their father's support. This initiative made it possible for all family members to express their sadness about the prospect of losing their wife and mother. Gloria reported a few painful occasions of crying together. She was pleased that this grief was balanced with some times of simply participating together in the normal routine of ongoing lives.

After the decision to not continue the chemotherapy, Gloria was able to enjoy being present at her grandson's thirteenth birthday in a much less anxious way. She was able to sit back and enjoy observing the occasion rather than experience the drain of her old pattern of trying to be close to Bronwyn. One month after the birthday gathering Gloria was admitted to hospital with severe abdominal pain. She went into a coma within 24 hours and died three days later. The speed of her collapse took her family by surprise but in many ways they were very prepared to grieve openly and support each other. Gloria had brought maturity into her family systems through her personal initiatives in her final year of life. Gloria had discussed funeral plans with each family member, which has assisted all the family, including her grandchildren, to play active parts in the service. She had shown that it is never too late to work on being more grown up. Gloria's efforts to balance dealing with her own health and relationship decisions and sharing support with others is an inspiring example of nurturing maturity.

Dealing with the inevitable in a grown-up way

With the advances in health care over the past decades the chances of us reaching old age are increasing. While life expectancy can be expanded, death is still an inevitable experience for all of us and our loved ones. Just as the young child does whatever it takes to stay at the park when their playtime is up, we adults have found lots of ways to avoid the reality of death. It is not uncommon for quite openly communicative families to close up around the subject of death, especially if the death is untimely. Moving out of our comfort zone to think and plan for how we want to deal with death and loss may well be one of the most maturing exercises we can take on. In the latter years of life, one challenge is to not be resigned to regrets about the past.

As the story of Gloria showed, it is not too late to change some of the ways we live our life and relationships. While it is unrealistic to expect that distant and tense relationships can magically be turned around in the latter phase of life, it's certainly possible to take some steps to bring a bit more maturity to important relationships. Remember that the work of growing up is always directed to our self, not to changing others. At every growing-up phase of life, there is opportunity to find enough inner strength to behave towards others in ways that reflect our values and beliefs rather than avoidant ways that express our insecurities.

Questions for reflection

» How has illness, death and loss been dealt with in the generations of my family?

» To what degree have feelings been cut off in order to cope? Or conversely, to what degree has moving on been swamped by immersion in feelings?

» What steps can I take to reconnect with important others while I have the time to do so?

» What principles do I want to guide me through ageing and facing the end of life?

» What aspects of my inner adult could use some attention right now?

» Think of a recent example of progress in applying the principles of growing up. Are there ways I can build on this?

From the inner child to the inner adult
Reflections on the lifelong journey of maturity

You have now managed to think through what it means to grow up, from the cradle to the grave, through all the stress points and opportunities that life presents. What a marathon effort to get this far! Having considered the growing-up phases of life, it's worth revisiting the qualities of leaving our inner child behind that were introduced at the beginning of this book. Core attributes of being a mature self in relationships are:

» Have your feelings without letting them dominate. Tolerate delays to being gratified.

» Work on inner guidelines. Refrain from blaming.

» Accept people with different views. Keep connected.

» Be responsible for solving your own problems. Let others have the space to solve theirs.

» Hold onto your principles, even when they won't win a popularity contest.

» Be able to see past yourself to the bigger picture of reactions and counter-reactions.

What do you think of these guidelines for even the most stressful of life's challenges? Can you see what maturity is like a little more clearly? More importantly, can you see the opportunities for growing up that are right before you? Have you seen glimpses of the difference you can make to yours and others' lives by taking on the challenge of being real about yourself in all relationships?

Epilogue

Society and self: the bigger picture of maturity

'The human is a narcissistic creature who lives in the present and who is more interested in his own square inch of real estate, and more devoted to fighting for his rights, than in the multigenerational meaning of life itself.'[1]

—Murray Bowen MD

I was struck by a newspaper article about an emerging world leader who was described as someone willing to listen to both sides and then make up his own mind. This was followed by the prediction that this nation might at last have a grown-up leader. I think this is a neat summary of being grown up in relationships: to be able to calmly listen to others but not be swayed by relationship forces in coming to a personal opinion. This book has primarily been about growing up in the context of our relationships but, of course, our relationship networks extend to our communities and how we live in our world. Think about the benefits to society at large if more people took on the growing-up challenge and saw their efforts to manage their anxiety and be principle-driven as a way of bringing more maturity to their society!

Getting past the desire for the quick-fix expert

A theme running all the way through this book is that clear thinking in the face of pressure increases our effectiveness. Each of us can discover that we have a surprising wealth of wisdom to draw on from our human brains that can help us resolve life's problems. The challenge is to put aside the desire for a quick fix and the tendency to look to others to come up with the instant solution. This quick-fix mentality has created a burgeoning industry of programs that promise a new method to get us out of our difficulties. Some even promise a new you in one week. Within my own profession of counselling and psychology, amidst some sound theories there are plenty of examples of this quick-fix technique trend.

Over my decades of clinical practice, I have observed that people make the best progress when they access their own answers to their dilemmas. I have learnt to refrain from giving directives and answers to client's difficulties and instead I endeavour to guide their focus away from changing or blaming others to looking at themself. I pay close attention to their descriptions of what they are doing to address their problems and ask them to assess what they think is helping and not helping. From here I can share some ideas about the predictable patterns that all humans get caught in when trying to manage the challenges of relationships. I then encourage clients to research these ideas in observing themselves in their real lives.

When people give up their own capacity to problem-solve, no matter what their intellectual capacity, they are left to either blindly depend on others or to blame and criticise others when their advice does not work. This leads to communities of dependent followers or reactive blamers.

When any one person pulls back from blaming others or trying to be the expert for others, or just going with the flow of others' opinions, it is possible to emerge as a more thoughtful, mature contributor to society.

Being mature in society

Most of the ideas in this book come from the theory developed by Dr Murray Bowen. One of his many poignant observations was that the same processes of immature relationships in families can be seen in society at large. Examples of this are everywhere. Think of the band-aid solutions being applied to relieve symptoms of our environmental misuse and consequential global warming. Efforts to logically examine a spectrum of reliable evidence and come up with ways to tackle the underlying causes of global warming are set aside in reaction to the pressure of powerful interest groups. As politicians and community leaders look for evidence that fits their own platform, they exaggerate the facts of both sides of the argument to capture the anxieties of the voting public. Just as when symptoms appear in our families, we are prone to responding with quick-fix solutions. We tend to focus on the symptoms as opposed to tackling the deeper contributions to the problem which involve making changes in ourselves.

One of the parallels that Bowen noticed between family and societal trends was the increasing focus on the next generation and the decreasing clarity of the adult generation. The focus on worrying about the next generation leaves both parents and policymakers increasingly confused about their own principles for reasonable and ethical behaviour. An over-focus on the next generation can contribute to their immaturity as they sense the uncertainty of the adults around them. Rather than respecting the principles of the older members of society, the younger generation feels pandered to and this increases their sense of entitlement. The school, government and legal systems can unknowingly get caught in this immaturity cycle by anxiously trying to 'fix' the young person who continues to lose responsibility and increases their helpless dependence on or rebellion towards the authorities. As with growing up in personal and family relationships, the most constructive effort on the stage of social responsibility is for people to examine their own contributions to collective problems, to clarify the principles they are willing to take a stand for, not push others to agree, and to work on themselves rather than to make a project out of other groups or the next generation.

The power of one

It's common to hear the view that the first step towards change in the world starts with changing yourself. At first hearing, this sounds great but it isn't at all straightforward. It's so much easier to pass the buck to others and then to blame and criticise our leaders when things don't go well rather than look at our own need to grow up. I like Dr Bowen's view of the challenge of growing up in the way we relate to our world at large. He described the human being as 'not willing to give up the easy life as long as there is a way to have his cake and eat it too'.[2] We all want healthier societies and families, but we are also prone to not want to tolerate the inconvenience of changing our behaviours that can contribute to this.

I don't want to be discouraging in wrapping up this book as there is so much that has been, and can be, achieved through an individual's efforts towards maturity. I think, however, it is healthy to be realistic about what we are up against in our efforts towards being grown up. We live in an increasingly anxious world. Band-aid solutions are no longer sufficient for the challenges of our environment, the conflict and polarisations between ethnic groups, severe food shortages, the breakdown of stable relationships, the deterioration of ethical behaviour in many sectors of society — and the list could go on.

Rather than become overwhelmed by such complications of human immaturity, there is an opportunity to be a pioneer in considering how our own behaviour may be part of the patterns that contribute to such problems. People who are willing to work on themselves and be the best that they can be in their communities can make a difference. Ripple effects flow from their progress in reducing their tendency to try to win the approval of others, or to cut off from relating to those who are different, or to try to fix others or label others as the cause of the problem. Such maturing people are not requiring validation from the wider society and are not thrown off course by others' criticism. They have grown up enough to know that operating at the best of one's capacity, while staying aware of their vulnerabilities, is sufficient to be a responsible citizen of their world.

Humility and maturity

I have made a choice in this book to focus on relationships among fellow humans. The ideas I have shared have been applied to and been beneficial in my own and many others' lives. As my life has progressed I have increasingly come to believe that the most important relationship to address in growing myself up is my relationship with the creator God. Not every reader will agree with this view but for me this keeps my self in perspective: as small and vulnerable, as well as graciously cared for. I think this has assisted in some way for me to reduce my natural self-centredness in relationships. Perhaps you might be prompted to venture your own thoughtful exploration of faith in your growing-up journey, but this decision would most helpfully come from within rather than from any pressure from another.

Holding onto one part of your inner child

While this book has encouraged you to leave behind the self-entitled inner child and to strengthen your inner adult in terms of principle-directed relational living, there is a part of childhood that is worth holding onto in the growing-up journey. This is the aspect of the child that snuggles into a parent's lap knowing he or she is vulnerable and dependent. For the adult this is called humility. It is the acceptance of frailty and the slow pace of our change efforts. It is the part of us that seeks beyond ourselves to find answers to the bigger questions of life's meaning.

One key aspect of Bowen theory that resonates for me is its humility, based on the observation that all of us have gaps in maturity. I think that Murray Bowen's theory has provided a gift to humanity in lending a hand to those who wish to bring some maturity to their relationships and their societies. At every stage of life, the familiar theme is that understanding ourselves in our families is crucial to being more of a grown-up in all our relationships.

A final word on growing up

Throughout this book I have drawn from my own life lessons and those of many people I have worked with in counselling. Their details have been changed to protect their identities but the stories of their lives have been real. I am indebted to the countless courageous people I have been privileged to work alongside in their efforts to grow themselves up. On the day I finished a draft of this book, I saw a woman in counselling who had come out of a difficult divorce and was struggling to juggle working part-time and raising three young children. She had been working on having more healthy relationships with each individual from her family of origin. Her progress was evident in that she was less dependent on her mother for approval and more able to voice her differences without backing away. Her comments at the end of our session provided the appropriate last word for this book.

She said: 'I can now see the kind of person I want to be — as a mother, a co-parent, a sister, a daughter and a friend. I can see who she is, but it's so hard to be this person.'

I asked her: 'Which of those roles is the hardest one for you to live out with the clear principles you've developed?'

Without hesitation she answered: 'The hardest one is how I am with myself. I'm hardest on myself. My criticisms and judgments can be so unreasonable. I know they don't fit the facts. But I'm getting a bit more "self" from inside me. I'm trying not to get it from others as much, and that has made such a difference.'

Being grown up is a lofty goal that is often frustratingly slow. Perhaps we don't have the capacity to be grown up in the way we like to imagine. One of the benefits of getting older is recognising that the hopes we invested in numerous schemes for fast self-improvement are not all they promised to be. Indeed, growing up in this anxious world and web of intense relationships isn't easy. At the same time, growing ourselves up just a notch means that our world looks vastly different and more promising, not just for ourselves but also for those we care about.

Appendix 1
Summary questions for reflection

The following is a review of core aspects in becoming more mature in life and relationships.

Using your mind alongside your feelings:
  » How much does my thinking guide my behaviour with others, or how much do I allow my feelings to take the lead?
  » How much am I able to be conscious of my feelings and to use them as a guide to the important issues I want to address?
  » To what extent am I focusing on the facts of the moment and not on feared possibilities?
  » To what degree am I able to observe and think about myself in my relationships as opposed to being caught up in an emotional experience?

Having well-developed guiding principles, instead of reacting to others:
  » How clear am I about my values, principles and goals as they apply to this particular situation?
  » How much am I aware of when I'm inconsistent with my principles to the detriment of myself and others?
  » To what degree am I able to keep my own counsel instead of finding allies to support me or villains to blame?

Seeing the interconnectedness of relationships:
  » How much am I caught up in my own needs and upsets in this situation instead of seeing what others are up against dealing

with how I'm reacting and behaving?

» To what degree am I blaming an individual and not seeing that each person contributes to the circuits of reactions in the group?

Keeping calm from the inside out:

» How well am I able to regulate or calm my worries, agitations and impulses from within, rather than from external distractions or from a relationship? Do I remember to breathe deeply?

» How consciously am I working at tolerating the discomfort that comes from choosing to step out of my and my system's comfort zone of predictable ways of relating?

Staying connected — especially in the face of difference:

» To what degree can I enjoy the mutual benefits of close relationships without losing my responsible self (my boundaries)?

» To what degree am I able to keep in calm contact with those in my family or group who view things differently to me?

» To what extent am I able to resist becoming a chameleon who adjusts my viewpoint to fit in with others and to keep a sense of peace?

» To what extent am I able to express my opinions without becoming emotionally charged up or needing to find allies to support my view?

Being able to function adequately across a range of life responsibilities:

» How much balance have I achieved across the various roles and responsibilities in my life?

» In how many areas of my life am I allowing others to fill my gaps instead of being responsible for myself?

» In how many areas of my life am I doing for others what they would benefit from learning to do for themselves?

Staying on course in the face of opposition from others in the system:

» To what extent do I stay with my chosen course of maturing myself when others are challenging me to go back to my predictable way of behaving?

» To what degree can I observe and accept how my own adjustments in becoming more responsible can be experienced for a time as destabilising for others?

Appendix 2

Mature connection and separateness

Becoming more relationally mature or differentiated requires finding a healthy balance of connection with others and separateness or autonomy from others. Connection and independence are equally important to work on. The following list illustrates what mature connection and autonomy may look like as opposed to connection and distancing efforts that are geared to reducing our fears and discomfort.

Mature connection

» Enjoying that we share some things in common.
» Friendship. Sharing things that are happening in our lives. Having fun together.
» Providing a sounding board: listening to each other's problems, allowing each person to work their own way through them. (Parents try not to involve children in issues of adult concern or problems that involve someone the child shares a relationship with.)
» Being interested in our different viewpoints.
» Cooperating with each other in practical ways.
» Treating each other with warmth and respect.
» Acts of kindness and affection.
» Being able to have disagreements.
» Being willing to ask for time together and being clear about what's important to us.

Exaggerated connection (fusion)

» Taking everything the other says personally. Reacting with attack, defence or hurt withdrawal.

» Needing the other to agree with us all the time.

» Expecting the other to solve our problems or make us feel good.

» Wanting the other to take our side against people with whom we have a conflict.

» Mind-reading the other. Completing their sentences. Interrupting. Assuming we know what they think.

» Thinking more about the relationship than our own responsibilities.

Mature separateness

» Having separate interests and friendships.

» Having different perspectives and points of view.

» Taking responsibility for our own needs and growth.

» Taking responsibility for our own problem-solving.

» Taking responsibility for calming our anxieties.

» Being able to ask for the space, privacy and respect we need.

Anxious separateness (cut off)

» Withdrawing contact when togetherness feels broken.

» Staying silent on our view because of fear of conflict.

» Believing that we can only be safe and happy by stopping all contact.

» Distancing without expressing our reasons.

» Making contact from a position of reluctant duty.

Appendix 3

What are guiding principles?

People with a reasonable level of differentiation (relational and emotional maturity) have put energy into using logical reasoning to form principles and convictions that they use to override the anxious charge in relationships during stressful situations.

Clarifying guiding principles that are useful in managing the day to day of relationship dilemmas is not an easy task. A principle is not an action but a belief about what is important to us and to the health of others in any given situation. An effort is made to draw on principles to guide behaviours rather than allow feelings and relationship pressures to shape actions. Ideally we develop these gradually over time through our own thinking, but in reality, most of us benefit from borrowing principles we hear from others and trying them out for ourselves. I don't expect that I will come close to completely measuring up to my chosen principles, especially when stress levels are high, but they provide me with a framework to reflect and work on. My life values are broader than my principles. They include living without false pride in reverence for God; and loving, respecting and being gracious to others as my fellow human beings.

The following are some ideas I have found very useful for guiding principles in my varied relationships:

» I am committed to not taking over and doing for another what they have the capacity to learn to do for themselves. (Not crowding another's breathing space so they can develop their own capabilities and coping skills.)

» I am committed to not expressing myself in a relationship without calming intense emotions to a level that allows me to be thoughtful.

» I am committed to sticking to what I am responsible for and not what is another's area of responsibility. (Not impinging on others' functioning.)

» I am committed to thinking, feeling, speaking and behaving on behalf of myself, not on behalf of another. (The 'I' position vs the 'You should' position.)

» I am committed to being as aware of another's interests as my own. I will endeavour to behave in ways that do not impair the growth of another.

» I am committed to putting energy into what's within my own control, not trying to change what is in others' control.

» I am committed to focusing on the part I am contributing to any relationship challenge and not focusing on critiquing or changing another. I will endeavour to ask myself, 'What is the other up against having to relate with me?'

» I am committed to hearing and understanding another's ideas before expressing my own.

» I am committed to following through on what I say I will take on and accepting responsibility for any lapses in my responsibility.

» I am committed to not inviting others to fill in my lapses in responsibility.

» I am committed to keeping problems in the relationship they belong in and not gossiping to others.

» I am committed to not saying anything about a person who is not present that I would not say if they were listening.

» I am committed to staying respectful and in contact with people who disagree with me.

» I am committed to checking that my feelings are in proportion to the facts of each situation.

» I am committed to consciously working on these principles in all my relationships and thinking through for myself whether or not they are sound.

Appendix 4

Differentiation of self as a continuum

The following is a summary of Dr Bowen's description of the characteristics of people at different levels of differentiation. We inherit our level of differentiation from the position we occupied, and the degree of maturity available, in the families we grow up in. Hence, we would do well to be realistic about where we are working from in endeavouring to increase out maturity. We are attracted to people with similar levels of differentiation. Any apparent variation in maturity in our intimate partnerships is likely to be a reflection of the loaning and trading of our pretend self. Relatively few people are in the higher levels of differentiation. (I don't view myself as being in this level but see it as a worthy set of characteristics to cultivate gradually!)

Lower scale people and groups are so overwhelmed by feelings that they struggle to see what is more factual and evidence based. Most of their energy goes into gaining love and approval in relationships or being angry at others when they don't provide it. There is no leftover energy for goal-directed behaviours. Their health and sense of wellbeing is dependent on relationships staying in balance. They may be highly dependent and accommodating with others, or moving from one relationship crisis to another. Decisions are made in a knee-jerk manner based on what feels right at the time. Long-term goals tend to be vague and feeling-laden, such as being happy, secure or successful.

Moderate scale people and groups sometimes have awareness of their thinking and values but tend to be sensitised to relationships so that opinions are avoided if there is risk of disapproval; or opinions get expressed with an exaggerated certainty and dogma. They can be well tuned to reading the body language, feelings and thoughts of others and can adjust themselves to be able to fit in with different groups. Success in life is often associated with receiving validation from others rather than from the value of the work done. Their self-esteem is prone to shift according to whether they receive compliments or criticism. Much energy goes into the pursuit of closeness which, if not achieved, can result in withdrawal and despondency.

Higher level people and groups can know the separation of their feelings and thinking, enabling them to state their beliefs calmly without insisting that they are right and others are wrong. They can freely choose when to be intimate and close with others and when to focus on goal-directed activity. They are realistic about their strengths and weaknesses. Their life path is determined more from within themselves rather than absorbed from what others think. They can be autonomous in close relationships and when they are on their own. They are able to be responsible for themselves and don't get into blaming others for their difficulties or crediting others for their successes. They can manage well in a broad range of situations, whether or not they are approved of by others.

Notes

Introduction
1 Empirical evidence for Bowen theory and differentiation of self:
» Charles, R. 2001, 'Is there any empirical support for Bowen's concepts of differentiation of self, triangulation, and fusion?', *American Journal of Family Therapy*, 29, pp. 279–92.
» Klever, P. 2009, 'Goal direction and effectiveness, emotional maturity, and nuclear family functioning', *Journal of Marital and Family Therapy*, 35, 3; pp. 308–24.
» Murdock, N.L. and Gore, P.A. 2004, 'Differentiation, stress, and coping: A test of Bowen theory', *Contemporary Family Therapy*, 26, pp. 319–35.
» Skowron, E.A. 2000, 'The role of differentiation of self in marital adjustment', *Journal of Counseling Psychology*, 47, pp. 229–37.
» Skowron, E.A., Stanley, K. and Shapiro, M. 2009, 'A longitudinal perspective on differentiation of self, interpersonal, and psychological wellbeing in young adulthood', *Contemporary Family Therapy*, 31, pp. 3–18.
» For examples of current research see The Family Systems Laboratory at Penn State University, Dept of Psychology: http://familysystemslab.psu.edu/

Chapter 1
1 Kerr, M.E. and Bowen, M. 1988, *Family Evaluation: An approach based on Bowen theory*, Norton, New York, p. 107.
2 Lerner, H. 1985, *The Dance of Anger: A woman's guide to changing the patterns of intimate relationships*, Harper & Row, New York, p. 40.

Chapter 2
1 Bowen, M. in Kerr, M.E. and Bowen, M. 1988, *Family Evaluation: An approach based on Bowen theory*, Norton, New York, p. 342.
2 Bowen, M. 1978, *Family Therapy in Clinical Practice*, Jason Aronson, New York, p. 365.
3 Checklist is drawn from descriptions of pseudo self and solid self in: Kerr, M.E. and Bowen, M. 1988, *Family Evaluation: An approach based on Bowen theory*, Norton, New York, pp. 104–105.

Chapter 3

1   Bowen, M. 1978, *Family Therapy in Clinical Practice*, Jason Aronson, New York, p. 492.
2   McGoldrick, M. 1995, *You Can Go Home Again: Reconnecting with your family*, Norton, New York, p. 32.

Chapter 4

1   Bowen, M. 1978, *Family Therapy in Clinical Practice*, Jason Aronson, New York, p. 383.
2   Carter, B. and Peters, J. 1996, *Love, Honor, and Negotiate: Making your marriage work*, Pocket Books, New York, p. 213.

Chapter 5

1   Bowen, M. 1978, *Family Therapy in Clinical Practice*, Jason Aronson, New York, p. 474.
2   Gilbert, R. 1992, *Extraordinary Relationships: A new way of thinking about human interactions*, John Wiley, New York, p. 158.

Chapter 6

1   Bowen, M. 1978, *Family Therapy in Clinical Practice*, Jason Aronson, New York, p. 475.
2   Schnarch, D. 1997, *Passionate Marriage: Love, sex, and intimacy in emotionally committed relationships*, Norton, New York, p. 49.

Chapter 7

1   Bowen, M. 1978, *Family Therapy in Clinical Practice*, Jason Aronson, New York, p. 280.
2   Schnarch, D. 1997, *Passionate Marriage: Love, sex, and intimacy in emotionally committed relationships*, Norton, New York, p. 78.

Chapter 8

1   Kerr, M. in Kerr, M.E. and Bowen, M. 1988, *Family Evaluation: An approach based on Bowen theory*, Norton, New York, p. 202.
2   Gilbert, R. 1999, *Connecting with Our Children: Guiding principles for parents in a troubled world*, John Wiley, New York, p. 11.
3   Stearns, P.N. 2003, *Anxious Parents: A history of modern childrearing in America*, New York University Press, New York.

Chapter 9

1 Bowen, M. 1978, *Family Therapy in Clinical Practice*, Jason Aronson, New York, p. 498.

2 Fox, L.A. and Gratwick-Baker, K. 2009, *Leading a Business in Anxious Times*, Care Communications Press, Chicago, p. 16.

3 Bowen, M. in Kerr, M.E. and Bowen, M. 1988, *Family Evaluation: An approach based on Bowen theory*, Norton, New York, pp. 342–3.

Chapter 10

1 Bowen, M. 1978, *Family Therapy in Clinical Practice*, Jason Aronson, New York, p. 473.

2 Ephesians Ch. 4:14, *The Bible*, New International version, Zondervan.

3 Wilson, D. 2007, 'A traditional wedding', *Credenda/Agenda*, vol. 9, 3. (Can be found at: www.reformedsingles.com; post 20 Jan 2009)

4 Dickson, J. 2004, *A Spectator's Guide to World Religions: An introduction to the big five*, Blue Bottle Books, Sydney, p. 15.

5 Menninger, K. 1973, *Whatever Became of Sin?* Hawthorn Books, New York.

Chapter 11

1 Bowen, M. 1978, *Family Therapy in Clinical Practice*, Jason Aronson, New York, p. 535.

2 Gilbert, R. 1992, *Extraordinary Relationships: A new way of thinking about human interactions*, John Wiley, New York, p. 157.

Chapter 12

1 Bowen, M. 1978, *Family Therapy in Clinical Practice*, Jason Aronson, New York, p. 305.

2 Gilbert, R. 1992, *Extraordinary Relationships: A new way of thinking about human interactions*, John Wiley, New York, p. 150.

3 Kerr, M.E. 2008, 'Why do siblings often turn out very differently?' in Fogel, A., King, B.J. and Shanker, S.G. (eds), *Human Development in the Twenty-first Century*, Cambridge University Press, London, pp. 206–15. Also available as a DVD from: www.thebowencenter.org

Chapter 13
1   Bowen M. in Kerr, M.E. and Bowen, M. 1988, *Family Evaluation: An approach based on Bowen theory*, Norton, New York, p. 343.
2   McGoldrick, M. 1995, *You Can Go Home Again: Reconnecting with your family*, Norton, New York, p. 276.

Chapter 14
1   Bowen, M. 1978, *Family Therapy in Clinical Practice*, Jason Aronson, New York, p. 494.
2   Papero, D. 1990, *Bowen Family Systems Theory*, Allyn & Bacon, Needham Heights, Massachusetts, p. 48.

Chapter 15
1   Bowen, M. 1978, *Family Therapy in Clinical Practice*, Jason Aronson, New York, p. 322.
2   Rosen, H.E. 2001, *Families Facing Death: A guide for healthcare professionals and volunteers*, Lexington Books, New York, p. 7.

Epilogue
1   Bowen, M. in Kerr, M.E. and Bowen, M. 1988, *Family Evaluation: An approach based on Bowen theory*, Norton, New York, p. 385.
2   Bowen, M. 1978, *Family Therapy in Clinical Practice*, Jason Aronson, New York, p. 281.

Bibliography and further reading

Bowen, M. 1978, *Family Therapy in Clinical Practice*, Jason Aronson, New York. (This book is a comprehensive collection of two decades of Bowen's research and papers.)

Carter, B. and Peters, J. 1996, *Love, Honor, and Negotiate: Making your marriage work*, Pocket Books, New York.

Cohn Bregman, O. and White, C.M. (eds) 2011, *Bringing Systems Thinking to Life: Expanding the horizons for Bowen family systems theory*, Taylor & Francis, New York.

Fox, L.A. and Gratwick-Baker, K. 2009, *Leading a Business in Anxious Times*, Care Communications Press, Chicago.

Gilbert, R.M. 2008, *The Cornerstone Concept: In leadership, in life*, Leading Systems Press, Falls Church, VA.

——2006, *Extraordinary Leadership: Thinking systems, making a difference*, Leading Systems Press, Falls Church, VA.

——2006, *The Eight Concepts of Bowen Theory: A new way of thinking about the individual and the group*, Leading Systems Press, Falls Church, VA.

——1999, *Connecting with Our Children: Guiding principles for parents in a troubled world*, John Wiley, New York.

——1992, *Extraordinary Relationships: A new way of thinking about human interactions*, John Wiley, New York.

Harrison, V. 2008, *My Family, My Self: A journal of discovery*, available at: www.csnsf.org

Herrington, J., Creech, R. and Taylor, T.L. 2003, *The Leader's Journey: Accepting the call to personal and congregational transformation*, John Wiley, New York.

Kerr, M. 2003, *One Family's Story: A primer on Bowen theory*, Bowen Center for the Study of the Family, www.thebowencenter.org

Kerr, M. and Bowen, M. 1988, *Family Evaluation: An approach based on Bowen theory*, Norton, New York.

Kerr, M.E. 2008, 'Why do siblings often turn out very differently?' in Fogel, A., King, B.J. and Shanker, S.G. (eds), *Human Development in the Twenty-first Century*, pp. 206–15, Cambridge University Press, London.

Lerner, H. 1988, *The Dance of Anger: A woman's guide to changing the patterns of intimate relationships*, Harper & Row, New York.

——1990, *The Dance of Intimacy: A woman's guide to courageous acts of change in key relationships*, Harper & Row, New York.

——2003, *The Dance of Connection: How to talk to someone when you're mad, hurt, scared, frustrated, insulted, betrayed, or desperate*, Harper & Row, New York.

McGoldrick, M. 1995, *You Can Go Home Again: Reconnecting with your family*, Norton, New York.

Miller, J. 2008, *The Anxious Organization: Why smart companies do dumb things*, Facts on Demand Press, Tempe, AZ.

Papero, D. 1990, *Bowen Family Systems Theory*, Allyn & Bacon, Needham Heights, Massachusetts.

Richardson, R. 2005, *Becoming a Healthier Pastor: Family systems theory and the pastor's own family*, Fortress Press, Minneapolis.

——1996, *Creating a Healthier Church: Family systems theory, leadership, and congregational life*, Fortress Press, Minneapolis.

——1995, *Family Ties that Bind: A self-help guide to change through family of origin therapy*, Self Counsel Press, Bellingham, WA.

Rosen, H.E. 2001, *Families Facing Death: A guide for healthcare professionals and volunteers*, Lexington Books, New York.

Schnarch, D. 1997, *Passionate Marriage: Love, sex, and intimacy in emotionally committed relationships*, Norton, New York.

Titelman, P. (ed.) 2008, *Triangles: Bowen family systems theory perspectives*, Haworth Clinical Practice Press, New York.

—— (ed.) 2003, *Emotional Cutoff: Bowen family systems theory perspectives*, Haworth Clinical Practice Press, New York.

—— (ed.) 1998, *Clinical Applications of Bowen Family Systems Theory*, Haworth Press, New York.

—— (ed.) 1987, *The Therapist's Own Family: Toward the differentiation of self*, Jason Aronson, Northvale, New Jersey.

Website resources

The Family Systems Institute Sydney, Australia: www.thefsi.com.au

The Bowen Center for the Study of the Family, Washington DC (links to other centres can be located on this site): www.thebowencenter.org

Acknowledgments

Many people and ideas have contributed to the evolution of this book. The most significant input comes from Dr Murray Bowen's brilliantly conceived theory of family systems. I consider myself fortunate to have come across this theory at the Family Institute of Westchester in 1992 and to have been able to draw from its keen observations and wisdom in the challenges and transitions of my life and my work. I am also indebted to those at the Bowen Center for the Study of the Family in Washington DC, under the leadership of Dr Michael Kerr, who have ensured that this theory continues to be applied, extended and made accessible. To my colleagues at the Family Systems Institute in Sydney, much of my learning in this book has been stimulated from your own commitment to learning and living Bowen theory. I am deeply indebted to my own family for the live learning they have given me of what it means (and how hard it can be) to be more responsible in my relationships. To my parents, Geoff and Judy, whom I have missed being able to share my adult life with, I am deeply grateful for their loving commitment to our family relationships. My sisters and brother, my husband and his family, and my two precious daughters are such an important part of my rich system of connections. You are all in the pages of this book for what you have taught me. A particular thankyou and loving appreciation to my husband David who has been my key supporter in this writing effort and has given me the necessary breathing space to maintain the project's momentum. To the many people I have worked alongside in my counselling practice, I am grateful for what you have taught me about systems and I have enormous respect for your perseverance in bringing your best to your lives and relationships. Your stories are central to bringing the thinking in this book to life.

Getting all of these ideas into a cohesive format has been a steep learning curve for me and I have benefitted from the help of some key people who have particular knowledge of what makes a jumble of stories and concepts into a useful book. Thanks to Joanne Corrigan and James Valentine for looking at my drafts and helping to resolve the identity crisis about the project's core message. My long-standing friend Jill Grundy has given her time to read and provide insightful feedback on the readability of the draft manuscript. This input, alongside her enthusiasm for the material, has been such a generous gift to me. And finally a thankyou to the team at Exisle Publishing, in particular Benny Thomas and Anouska Jones, who believed that this material had something unique to offer and have polished it up to become a real book.

Index

A

abandonment experience 41
abuse
  communicating experience 62–3
acceptance
  two-way 189
adolescents *see* teenagers
adults *see* inner adult; mature adults;
  single young adults
affairs, midlife 192–4
ageing well 197–205, 214
anxiety
  body's response to 75
  calming own 83
  child's response 114–15
  external distracters 77–8
  focus of parents 173–4
  learning self-regulation 74–5
  lessons on 72–5
  relationship dependence 174–9
  single young adults 67
  stress-relieving patterns 181
  in workplace 147–8
apologising
  to indigenous Australians 157–8
  mature contrition 158–9
approval
  need for 176–7, 185
  seeking 29–32
  'togetherness approval' 30
  using sex 99–100
atheism, Western world 156
authenticity as goal 63–4
autonomy within marriage 88
awareness, two levels of 158–9

B

balance
  maintaining 44
  in marriage 93–4, 102
  within relationships 88–90
  work–life 28–9, 141, 146
belief systems
  examination of 155–6
beliefs
  developing 150–60, 161
  examination of 151–2
  family's traditions 152–3
  independent from family 159–60
  pretend maturity 33–4
  problems with borrowing 153–5
  superficial 151
blame cycle
  marriage breakup 166–8
blaming
  getting beyond 49
  others 1, 11–12
  parents 40
  refraining from 17
  self 2, 12
'borrowing' maturity 30–5
Bowen, Dr Murray 4, 217
Bowen family systems theory
  background 3–5
  emotional health 174
  overview 47–8
  societal trends 218
brain development 20–1
bravado, pretend 33

C

cancer
  chemotherapy 211–12
  death of mother 206–7
  effect on relationship 175
  family relationships 210–12
  see also death
caretaker role
  caring for disabled daughter 182–4
  within marriage 89
  pulling back from 76–7
  stresses of 75–7
'change back!' reactions 76–7
'changing the other person' fantasy
  83–5
chemotherapy 211–12
childhood
  immaturity *see* inner child
  relationship language of 15–16
children
  becoming adult 199–200
  brain development 20
  developmental environment changes
    107–8
  effect on marriage 91–2
  eldest 117–18
  healthy connection with 115–17
  with learning delays 112–13
  over-focus on 218
  over-involved parents 108–15
  response to anxiety 114–15
  shifting focus off 94–5
  see also inner child
chocolate, saying no to 70
code of ethics, conscious 159–60
commitment phobia 40–5
conflict cycle
  breaking 93–4, 167–8
conflict/distance dance 87–8
connection

healthy parent–child 115–17
  within marriage 86–7
  mature 116
  with others 72–5
  out-of-proportion 116
  workplace balance 146
contact
  after divorce 170–1
  after leaving home 60–1
  maintaining with others 178
  see also connection
contrition
  mature 158–9
conviction/connection workplace
  balance 146
coping patterns 47
couples counselling 95
courtship
  early phases 82
cut-off behaviour *see* distancing
  behaviour

D

death
  avoiding reality 212–13
  denial about imminence 206–7
  family decisions 211–12
  of mother 206–8
  of parents 32
  preparing for 208–12
  questions for reflection 214
  shutting down feelings 207–8
dependence
  on parents 55–6
  in relationships 174–9, 180–1
depression
  relationship dependence 174–9
Dickson, John 156
differentiation
  as a continuum 173–4
  of self 4–5, 47
  staying realistic 184–5

disabled child, caring for 182–4
disagreements 18
disappointments, large 182
discipline techniques 119–20
distance/conflict dance 87–8
distancing behaviour
    from disapproval 176
    emotional cut-off 48
    in face of challenge 138–40
    facing death 206–8
    between family members 48
    father's 43
    within marriage 76, 86
    from parents 55–60
    separation struggle 167
    during sex 100
    stress-relieving pattern 181
    of team leader 142–5, 146
distractions
    external, as substitutes 67, 77–8
divorce 165–71
    emotional vs legal 168–70
    questions for reflection 171
    shared parenting 169–70
dogmatism 153–5

E
early abandonment experience 41
Ed and Linda's story 108–13
emotional cut-off *see* distancing
    behaviour
emotional discomfort 23
emotional intimacy
    transferred 192–4
empty nest adjustment 201–2
entrapment, sense of 183–4

F
families
    balance with work 141
    behaviour within 4–5
    confronting imminent death 210–12
    reconnecting with 200–1

    see also family of origin
family dynamics
    examples of patterns 37–8
    questions for reflection 50
    relationship with parents 42–3
family of origin
    painful, unhappy 62–3
    reconnecting with 60–1, 200–1
    understanding 37–49
family projection process 47–8
family systems concepts 47–8
fathers
    death of father 32
    distancing behaviour by 43
    as role models 68–71
fault finding 1–2
fitting in 15–16
friendships 78–9
fusion
    with children 116
    between the emotional/intellectual
        172
    family togetherness 47
    workplace 146

G
Gloria's story, preparing for death
    208–12
'go slow' approach 24
gossiping 142
grandparenting pitfalls 202–4
gratification
    childhood need for 15
    with food 70
    instant 14
    self-gratification 190
    tolerating delay 17
Greg's story 40–5
grief
    making a project of 183
    midlife regrets 195–6
group ethos 15–16, 20, 33

growing up
   being more real 176–9
   biology of 20–1
   learning from the child 16
   midlife challenge 189–91
   paradox of marriage 95–6
   questions for reflection 65
   relationally 21–2
   see also leaving home; maturity
guilt
   unhealthy 158–9

H

humility 220–1

I

'I' position 120–3, 128
indigenous Australians, public apology
   to 157–8
individuality
   loss of 83–4
   within marriage 86–7
   in relationships 11–13, 30
in-laws
   grandparenting difficulties 202–4
   tension about 91–2
inner adult
   in the bedroom 100–4
   growing 14–16
   solid, characteristics 34
inner child
   discovering 14–16
   under relationship pressure 13
inner thinking guidance system 159–60

J

Jerry's story 27–9

L

language
   childhood relationships 15–16
Larissa's story 57–60
Laura and Gavin's story 191–4
leadership
   mature characteristics 146–7
   roles 31

learning delays
   dealing with 112–13
leaving home
   after abuse 62–3
   healthy transition 53–5
   maintaining contact 60–1
   ongoing issues 61–2
   questions for reflection 65
   spectrum of dependence 55–6
life stages 7–8

M

marriage
   autonomy within 88
   blame cycle 166–8
   breakup 28–9
   bringing childish myths to 82–6
   choice of ceremony 152–3
   growing-up paradox of 95–6
   midlife crisis 191–4
   open arrangement 98
   questions for reflection 96
   readiness for 81–2
   reconnecting in retirement 198–201
   re-focusing of partners 111
   requirements within 28
   three 'maturity detours' 86–95
   triangle patterns 91–2
marriage dance patterns
   changing 85–6
   examples 82–5
   interrupting 92–3
mature adults
   attributes 17–19
   characteristics 19
   managing feelings 17
maturity
   as a continuum 173–4, 179–80
   core attributes 215
   'go slow' approach 24
   guidelines for strengthening 178–9
   and humility 220–1
   inconsistent 13, 27–9

questions for reflection 25, 36, 186
superficial 34
symptoms and setbacks 172–86
see also pretend maturity; real
   maturit
'maturity detours'
in marriage 86–95
maturity gaps
filled by others 71–2
filled by partner 84
midlife exposure 191–4
in the workplace 133–48
Menninger, Dr Karl 157
mental health theories 174
midlife
affairs 192–4
crisis or opportunity 189–96
exposing maturity gaps 191–4
losing security props of youth 194–6
questions for reflection 196
mind-reading delusion 83
multigenerational transmission
   process 48

N

next generation, over-focus on 218
nuclear family emotional system 47

O

older age 197–205, 214
one-up one-down pattern 88–90, 94,
   102, 175
only child 39
open marriage arrangement 98
out-of-proportion connection 116
over-controlling
at workplace 136–7
over-responsibility, workplace 135
overworking cycle 134, 135–7

P

parent–child relationship
circular dance 114–15
idealised bond 115

individual parents 127–8
tensions in adult life 61–2
parenthood
impact of 117–18
parenting
after divorce 169–70
anxieties about ability 109–10
changing techniques 124–6
checklist 127–8
different styles 126–8
effect of marriage tensions 106–7
facing own immaturity 123
overly focusing on children 108–15
questions for reflection 129
re-focusing on self 108–13
today's challenges 107–8
parents
caring for vs caretaker 57–60
death of 32, 206–8
dependence of children 55–6
filling children's gaps 72
influence on children 38
own maturity pathway 40, 60–1
re-establishing contact with 177
siblings' relationships with 42–3
understanding their relationship
   42–3
partnering
society's emphasis on 70–1
partners
filling maturity gap 84
persona
public and private 27, 29
personal responsibility 157–8
power of one 219–20
pretend bravado 33
pretend maturity 26–35
borrowing maturity 30–5
characteristics checklist 33
pros and cons 27
values 33–4

principles
  inner guidelines 17
  maintaining own 18–19
  pretend maturity 33–4
  strong set of 159–60
problem-solving
  immature pattern 136–7
  for others 23
  own problems 18, 217
promotion in workplace 142–5
psychology
  diverging with faith 157
public persona 27, 29
punishments
  with children 120–2
  puppy management 119
puppy management 119–20
Q
questions for reflection
  ageing well 205
  developing mature beliefs 161
  family dynamics 50
  grown-up parenting 129
  leaving home and growing up 65
  marriage 96
  maturity assessment 25, 36
  maturity symptoms and setbacks 186
  midlife 196
  old age and facing death 214
  separation and divorce 171
  sex for grown-ups 105
  for single young adults 80
  work and workplace 149
quick-fix mentality 216–7, 218
R
reactions
  and counter-reactions 19
real, being 176–9
real maturity 26–35
  characteristics checklist 34–5
  facing relationship challenges 30
  questions for reflection 25, 36, 186

rebellion 33
reconnection
  with family 63–4, 200–1
  see also connection
regrets
  dealing with 196
  midlife 195–6
relationship maturity
  looking at self 12–13
relationship systems 3
relationship triangles 44–6
relationships
  adult 16
  avoiding tension 29–30
  balance within 88–90
  filling maturity gaps 66–71
  health-enhancing 69–71
  laboratory for growing up 22–3
  maintaining balance 44
  as a mutual exchange 79
  reconnecting with family 200–1
  as a security blanket 66–7
  as a sedative 75
  seeing patterns 3
  sensitivity to 179–81
  strains of dependency 180
  tackling dependence 175–9
  types of dependency 180–1
remorse, genuine 158–9
resentment build-up, own part in 183–4
resilience
  borrowed 175–6
responsibilities
  gaps in managing 71–2
  imbalance in marriage 93–4, 102
  personal and social 157–8
retirement 198–9
rewards
  with children 120–3
  puppy management 119
Rhonda's story 68–71
Richard's story 138–40

right and wrong, concept of 157, 159
romantic love
    early phases 82
Rudd, Prime Minister Kevin
    showing responsibility 157–8
running away from family home 55–6
S
saying sorry *see* apologising
school drop-off time 107
self
    abdicating responsibility 177, 217
    'borrowed' sense of 31–2
    differentiation of 4–5
    projection on partner 84
    refocusing on 111
    see also individuality
self-blame 12
self-focus 19
self-gratification 190
self-management *see* self-regulation
self-promotion 2
self-reflection
    midlife 194–6
self-regulation
    focus on 177–9
    learning self 74–5
    teenagers' learning 123–6
separation 165–71
    blame cycle 166–8
    managing mature parenting 167–8
sex
    for personal validation 99–100
sex life
    avoidance of other issues 98–9
    avoidance of sex 97–8, 102–3
    'just do it' motto 103
    questions for reflection 105
    repairing 100–4
sexual expression, mature 104–5
sibling position
    eldest 117–18
    only child 39

relationally formative 48
siblings
    different family experiences 38–9,
        42–3
Simon's workplace challenges 142–6
single young adults 66–79
    anxiety 67
    beneficial practices 67–8
    leaving-home transition 78–9
    questions for reflection 80
singleness 70–2, 78–9
social responsibility 157–8
societal regression process 48
societal trends 218
spiritual faith *see* beliefs
Stearns, Peter 108
stress
    self-regulation 74–5
stress-relieving patterns 181
superficial maturity 34
'surface-level' adult *see* pretend
        maturity
T
taking over others' tasks 18
tantrums, toddler's 14
teenagers
    brain development 20–1
    learning self-regulation 123–6
    social needs 16
'togetherness approval' 30
'togetherness' fusion, workplace 146
tree root damage 85
triangle positions 45–6
triangles
    around daughter-in-law 204
    de-triangling strategies 144–5
    dismantling 95
    family facing death 211–12
    loss at retirement 200
    within marriage 91–2
    in relationships 44–6
    workplace 142–5

U

under-functioning
   steps to maturity 140
   at workplace 137–40
under-responsibility, workplace 135–40
unfairness
   dealing with 182–4
university studies
   choices of discipline 31–2

V

validation *see* approval
values
   inner guidelines 17
   pretend maturity 33–4
views
   accepting differences 18

W

'what if' fears 73–4
'what now' worries 73–4
withdrawal
   cycle at work 138–40
   see also distancing behaviour
work–life balance 28–9, 141
workplace
   anxiety in 147–8
   connection/conviction balance 146
   de-triangling strategies 144–5
   over-controlling at 136–7
   over-functioning at 199–200
   over-responsibility at 135
   questions for reflection 148–9
   tension from promotion 142–5
   triangles at 142–5
worries
   imagined 73–4
wrongdoing
   being honest about 158
   denying 157